Henry Cotterill

Does Science Aid Faith in Regard to Creation?

Henry Cotterill

Does Science Aid Faith in Regard to Creation?

ISBN/EAN: 9783337035839

Printed in Europe, USA, Canada, Australia, Japan

Cover: Foto ©Lupo / pixelio.de

More available books at **www.hansebooks.com**

DOES SCIENCE AID FAITH IN REGARD TO CREATION?

BY THE RIGHT REV.
HENRY COTTERILL, D.D., F.R.S.E.,
BISHOP OF EDINBURGH,
FORMERLY BISHOP OF GRAHAMSTOWN, AND SOMETIME FELLOW
OF ST. JOHN'S COLLEGE, CAMBRIDGE.

London:
HODDER AND STOUGHTON,
27, PATERNOSTER ROW.
MDCCCLXXXIII.
[All rights reserved.]

"Almighty God, who hast created man in Thine own Image, and made him a living soul that he might seek after Thee, and have dominion over Thy creatures, teach us to study the works of Thy hands, that we may subdue the earth to our use, and strengthen our reason for Thy service; and so to receive Thy blessed Word, that we may believe on Him whom Thou hast sent, to give us the knowledge of salvation and the remission of our sins. All which we ask in the name of the same Jesus Christ our Lord."

James Clerk Maxwell (1831—1879).

"Thou, O Father, who gavest the visible Light as the first-born of Thy creatures, and didst pour into man the intellectual light as the top and consummation of Thy workmanship, be pleased to protect and govern this work, which coming from Thy goodness returneth to Thy glory. Thou, after Thou hadst reviewed the works which Thy hands had made, beheldest that everything was very good, and Thou didst rest with complacency in them. But man, reflecting on the works which he had made, saw that all was vanity and vexation of spirit, and could by no means acquiesce in them. Wherefore, if we labour in Thy works with the sweat of our brows, Thou wilt make us partakers of Thy vision and Thy Sabbath. We humbly beg that this mind may be steadfastly in us; and that Thou, by our hands, and also by the hands of others, on whom Thou shalt bestow the same Spirit, wilt please to convey a largess of new alms to Thy family of mankind. These things we commend to Thy everlasting love, by our Jesus, Thy Christ, God with us. Amen."

Bacon (1561—1626).

ANALYTICAL TABLE OF CONTENTS.

                                                  PAGE

INTRODUCTION 3-8

PART I.

THE CHRISTIAN FAITH ON THE SUBJECT OF CREATION.

CHAPTER I.

APOSTOLIC DEFINITION 11-22

First Article of the Christian Faith—First Principle in all Religion—In Heb. xi. 3, definition of the Faith as derived from Genesis—The Æons here the Days of Creation—The *Word* the Agent in Creation—Language of Genesis Symbolic—Purpose of the Sacred History.

CHAPTER II.

HISTORY OF CREATION NOT SCIENTIFIC . . 23-32

Religious Value of Faith as to Creation—The History given for Man, and therefore not Scientific—Speaks of Causes beyond Human Knowledge, and therefore only describes Results—Could not use the Language of Physical Science because such Language never can be the Whole Truth—Instance as regards Creation of Light.

CHAPTER III.

GOD'S GLORY IN CREATION 33-46

Creation of Light first act in Creation, because of Relation of Light to Visible Universe—Light medium of Communication between the Creation and Reason—First Day, therefore the Lord's Day—Light represents to man God's glory—Reveals it to the Spirit of Man—"The Lilies of the Field"—The Rainbow—But Beauty of Nature cannot of itself teach Religion.

CHAPTER IV.

CREATION THE WORK OF WISDOM . . . 47-55

False idea of God as mere Power—Old Testament teaches that Creation by Wisdom—Definition of Wisdom—Creation described in Book of Job—Wisdom of God in Creation infinitely beyond that of man, both in kind and in degree—Practical application to Human Life.

CHAPTER V.

REASON THE LIGHT OF DIVINE WISDOM . . 56-62

Relation of Human Reason to Divine Wisdom indicated both in the Old and in the New Testament—Wisdom in the Proverbs intellectual as well as moral—Illustrated in Solomon—The Divine Wisdom includes, while it infinitely surpasses, all Human Knowledge and Science—St. John, in his teaching as to the *Logos*, confirms this.

CHAPTER VI.

TEACHING OF ST. AUGUSTINE 63-75

Charge that the Religious view of Creation has been adjusted to suit discoveries of modern Science—True as regards some

Analytical Table of Contents. vii

post-Reformation Theology—But completely answered by the views held by Early Christian writers, ages before the birth of modern Science—St. Augustine—Prepared for this work by his experience of Manichæism—His first work on Genesis against the Manichæans treats the History as an Allegory—Yet contains the idea of Creation being analogous to the Evolution of a Plant out of a Seed, which he expounded in subsequent Works—His wise cautions against bringing our conclusions from Scripture into conflict with the conclusions of Science—Creation of the physical causes which in due order produced all Nature is the Creation of Natural things.

CHAPTER VII.

TRUE IDEA OF CREATION 76-81

The Creator present always in His Works—Every Man born into the World as much the Creation of God as Adam—The Hundred and Fourth Psalm a complete Exposition of this truth—Creation in several distinct senses—Primary Creation—Secondary or derivative Creation—But period before the Creation of man to be distinguished from that which follows.

CHAPTER VIII.

CREATION SUBJECTED TO VANITY . . . 82-95

Teaching of St. Paul as to Creation in Romans viii.—$\kappa\tau i\sigma\iota\varsigma$ illustrated from Revelation v.—"Vanity" from the Book of Ecclesiastes—Connection of the Argument in Romans viii. with that of the fifth Chapter, and with the History of the Fall—Because in the order of the Divine counsels, Redemption preceded Creation—Hooker and St. Augustine—Further illustrations from Scripture—The present state of Creation provisional.

PART II.

SCIENTIFIC ASPECTS OF CREATION.

CHAPTER I.

SCIENCE INTERPRETS DIVINE WISDOM IN CREATION 99-105

St. Paul's argument as to the manifestation of God in His works implies that Science must aid Faith if it fulfils its true functions—It confirms the Witness to God in the unity, order, and causation of the Universe—Mistaken attitude of Theologians towards Science—Result that Science regarded as natural adversary of Faith—Sir W. Hamilton—"Unseen Universe"—True Relation between Faith and Science.

CHAPTER II.

PRIMARY CREATION BEYOND SCIENCE . . 106-114

Objection to Christian Faith in regard to Creation as "unthinkable"—Every theory of Creation equally so—Objection as to break of Continuity—Creation the Relation both of the finite to the Infinite, and of Reason to external World—Is the visible Universe a Physical or Spiritual production?

CHAPTER III.

LAW IN CREATION 115-123

Both Science and Theology have Law as a fundamental Principle—Hooker on Law of Nature—Must be Law of Wisdom—Is it Unchangeable or Arbitrary?—In the view of Science Unchangeable—Such Law necessary for rational Beings—True Meaning of *Law*—Distinction between Phenomenal and Dynamical Law.

Analytical Table of Contents.   ix

CHAPTER IV.

IMMENSITY OF CREATION 124-129

Number of Stars—Magnitudes and Distances of Heavenly Bodies—Mind obtains no Idea of these except by Comparison—Sirius—Distance and Mass—Apparently a "Giant Sun" of "Giant Planets"—Do these Discoveries aid Faith or overwhelm it?

CHAPTER V.

LIFE IN OTHER WORLDS 130-142

General Belief fifty years ago — Discoveries of Astronomy counterbalanced by those of Geology in respect to other Worlds being abodes of rational Life—Whewell on "Plurality of Worlds"—His Statement of Argument from Geology—Man the climax of Creation—Question affected by Discoveries of "spectrum analysis," and by Laws of Transformation and Conservation of Energy—Proctor's view—Conclusion founded on Assumptions respecting which Science gives no Information — But does not affect Faith in regard of Creation.

CHAPTER VI.

LAW OF EVOLUTION 143-159

The growth of a Plant from its Seed, by which Augustine illustrated Creation, the process in Nature from which the Law of Evolution derived—Principles of that Law, and Definition—The same Law fulfilled in the growth of a Chick in an Egg and in the birth of an Infant—In the System of the Universe—In the Earth's Structure—This Law, in its largest sense, the order through which Creation effected—The same order exhibited in the System of Animal Life—Confirmed by the teaching of Embryology.

CHAPTER VII.

EVOLUTION OF THE INORGANIC UNIVERSE . . 160-173

That Inorganic Nature was constituted through Physical Causes not supposed to be inconsistent with a Divine Creator—Nebular Theory—Sir William Thomson's Theory—General Scientific considerations suggested by Jevons—Prove that Will of the Creator cannot be excluded by Science, nor the causes explained through which the Evolution effected—Constitution of the Matter of which Universe composed—Atomic Theory—Molecules, differently arranged Systems of Elementary Atoms—Conjectural order of development of the Material of the Visible Universe—General conclusion as to development of the Inorganic Universe agrees with Law of Evolution.

CHAPTER VIII.

ORGANIC NATURE 174-193

Agassiz and Huxley on Characteristics of *Life*—Science, both Experimental and Theoretical, denies Spontaneous Generation—Definition of Evolution of each individual organism—Chief cause of Evolution unknown and mysterious—"Natural Selection" and "Survival of fittest"—Darwin, Mivart, and Lubbock—Two objections fatal to Natural Selection being the true cause of the Evolution of Organic Nature—General definition of that Evolution—Important inference from the Analogy of Embryology.

CHAPTER IX.

CREATION OF MAN 194-200

Creation of Man twofold—Perfection of Animal Nature; and Living Soul—The latter immediate Creation—Science confirms this—Negative Evidences—Positive—Man' ritual Being belongs to Eternity.

CHAPTER X.

LAW OF DECAY 201-208

Argument from Design strengthened by Science—But that Argument sometimes Illogical—Wisdom seeks best ends—Ideas of Modern Theology as to Creation—Corrected by Geology—Laplace's proof of Stability of Planetary System—Later discoveries of Science—"Degradation of Energy" proves that Law of Decay is Universal.

CONCLUSION 209-216

APPENDIX 217-228

INTRODUCTION.

INTRODUCTION.

THE purpose of this treatise cannot be better described than by referring to an eloquent and suggestive passage in the Inaugural Address, at the Church Congress held at Newcastle in 1881, by its President, the Bishop of Durham. In that year the British Association for the Advancement of Science had lately celebrated its jubilee in the metropolitical city of York, where, fifty years before, it had its birth.

"The President of that Association" (the Bishop observed) "availed himself of the occasion to sum up the achievements of the half-century past,—untrodden fields opened out, fresh sciences created, a whole world of fact and theory discovered, of which men had hardly a suspicion at the beginning of this period. In this commemoration we are reminded of the revolution in the intellectual world which has taken place in our time, as in the other" (the centenary of the birth of Stephenson) "our attention was directed to the revolution in the social and industrial world. Here again we are confronted with a giant force, of which the Church of Christ must give account. If we are wise, we shall endeavour to understand and absorb these truths. They are our proper heritage as Christians, for they are manifestations of the Eternal Word, who is also the Head of the Church. They will add breadth and strength and depth to our theology. Before all things we shall learn by the lessons of the past to keep ourselves free from any distrust or dismay. Astronomy once menaced, or was thought to menace, Christianity. Long before we were born, the menace had passed away. We found astronomy the sworn ally of religion. The heresy of the fifteenth and sixteenth centuries had become the orthodoxy of the nineteenth. When some years ago an eminent man of science, himself a firm believer, wrote a work throwing doubt on the plurality of worlds, it was received with a storm of adverse criticism, chiefly from Christian teachers, because he ventured to question a theory which three centuries earlier it would have been a shocking heresy to maintain. Geology next entered the lists. We are old enough, many of us, to remember the anxiety and distrust with which its startling announcements were received. This scare, like the other, has passed away. We admire the providential design which through myriads of years prepared the earth by successive gradations of animal and vegetable life for its ultimate destination as the abode of man. Nowhere else do we find more vivid and striking illustrations of the increasing purpose which runs through the ages. Our theological conceptions have been corrected and enlarged by its teaching, but the work of the Church of Christ goes on as before. Geology, like astronomy, is fast becoming our faithful ally. And now, in turn, Biology concentrates the same interests, and excites the same distrusts. Will not history repeat itself? If the time should come when evolution is translated from the region of suggestive theory to the region of acknowledged fact, what then? Will it not carry still further the idea of providential design and order? Will it not reinforce with

Introduction. 5

new and splendid illustrations the magnificent lesson of modern science—complexity of results traced back to simplicity of principles, variety of phenomena issuing from unity of order—the gathering up, as it were, of the threads which connect the universe, in the right hand of the One Eternal Word?" (*Official Report of Church Congress*, 1881, pp. 15, 16.)

Are these descriptions of the history of the past relations between Christianity and Science in all respects true? Or even granting this, can we admit that the sanguine anticipations as to their future relations are equally trustworthy? On both these grounds, the view here presented to us in the fervid language of the Bishop has been challenged. It is maintained by the adversaries of orthodox Christianity, who urge it as a proof that the religion itself is changing its form as mankind becomes enlightened; even by some of its adherents it is admitted, but only as a sufficient reason for distrusting science itself, as the philosophy by which men are led astray from the simplicity of faith in Christ; that although it may be true that, as science has made its discoveries, theologians have contrived to adjust their belief to the new views that have been forced upon them much against their own will, and thus to satisfy themselves, though they have not satisfied the world in general; at all events they have never effected such adjustment, without a serious loss to Christianity itself, at least as accepted by them; the loss of a belief in Scripture as really inspired by God, and therefore perfectly and absolutely true according to that interpretation of it which an honest and impartial mind must accept. If it is a "nose of wax," to be twisted to one side and the other by a process of accommodation to suit new views of truth; or to be explained away to mean the very opposite of that which it seems to mean;

what will be the result of such a process, but that Christianity itself, with all its supernatural dogmas, will ultimately disappear? And further as regards the future, it is confidently asserted that the new discoveries, especially in the direction of evolution, are to give, if they have not already given, the death-blow to the whole system of supernatural religion.

The present treatise, which discusses the momentous question how the Christian faith on the subject of Creation is affected by the progress of physical science, is written, it need hardly be said, from the Christian or theological standpoint, not the scientific. Nor does it profess to be a work on the evidences of Christianity. It is intended for those that believe, not for those that believe not. Its purpose is to quicken and strengthen the faith of those, who have found the spiritual truth which is revealed in Christ to be the Light and Life of their souls, by assisting them to recognise more distinctly what is the relation of revealed truth to such other truth as the enlightened reason of man can discover in nature. It is indeed obvious, to every one who is capable of reflecting at all on the question, that the truth that is indeed revealed from God, and that which the Divine gift of reason enables man to conclude from God's own works—so that the conclusions cannot be denied without denying reason itself—cannot possibly contradict one another, whatever they may seem to do. But as these two kinds of truth lie in different spheres of man's being, and address different faculties,—the distinction between them being, at least, as wide as that between *science* and *art* (for example), or even that between material *quantity* and moral *quality*,—it is easy to see that the language in which the one kind of truth is conveyed to the human mind, may be, or rather we should say, *must be*, very different from that which is necessary to express the other. How differently, for example, would the very same scene in nature be described by the physicist and by the artist,—or, much more, by the poet; so that often there might be apparent contradiction where there is none in reality. We need not therefore be surprised if Holy Scripture, in which God reveals Himself to us in order that we may obtain that eternal life which consists in the knowledge of Him, and of Jesus Christ whom He has sent, uses very different language on many subjects from that which would be employed if its purpose were to convey scientific knowledge. Even as a poet's description of some natural phenomenon, which might be perfectly true from the aspect in which he regarded it, might yet produce utterly incorrect impressions on the mind of one ignorant of science, as to the physical causes to which the effects He described were due; so, and much more, when Holy Scripture represents Creation as the work of the Infinite God, and in its relation to man and his duty to God his Maker, we might expect with confidence—as experience has shown to have been the case in time past—that ideas would be produced as to the physical character of that work, which could only take the forms into which our previous knowledge enabled us to interpret the language. These would become necessarily modified as our knowledge of the physical universe advanced, and corrected the inaccurate and imperfect interpretations. And thus science may seem, as it progresses, to be opposed to revelation, and to contradict its teachings; and it will for a season supply arguments to its adversaries, simply because it corrects those notions which were all our previous ignorance allowed us to form. Ultimately, however, when we discover that our interpretations of the language have all the while obscured the underlying truth, instead of being part of it, or at all essential to it, the discoveries of science are, in their permanent results, nothing but gain to real Christianity.

This general view of the question is one that readily presents itself to every thoughtful and impartial mind, which is, at the same time, profoundly convinced of the reality of that spiritual truth which Holy Scripture reveals, and also conscious that the reason of man, to which God Himself appeals in His word, is not given to mislead and deceive us when we study His works in nature, His own creation. All that is proposed in this treatise is to illustrate this general view in some of the more important aspects of the subject.

For the more distinct exposition of the argument, the work is divided into two parts, of which the first discusses at length the Christian Faith in regard to Creation, with the special view of exhibiting it, not merely as a dogma, but as a rational belief, consistent with all the perfections of God, and with the other doctrines of the Catholic religion. The second part touches on some of the scientific aspects of Creation. It would not be suitable to a theological work, nor would it be possible within the limits of this treatise, to enter in any detail into an examination of all the various scientific questions which bear more or less directly on the subject of Creation as apprehended in the Faith of the Church. It will be sufficient in that part to give some illustrations of that harmony between Science and Faith, which is the result of each observing the limits of the legitimate sphere which God has ordained for each.

PART I.

THE CHRISTIAN FAITH ON THE SUBJECT OF THE CREATION.

CONTENTS OF PART I.

CHAP. I. APOSTOLIC DEFINITION.
,, II. HISTORY OF THE CREATION NOT SCIENTIFIC.
,, III. GOD'S GLORY IN CREATION.
,, IV. CREATION THE WORK OF WISDOM.
,, V. REASON THE LIGHT OF DIVINE WISDOM.
,, VI. TEACHING OF ST. AUGUSTINE.
,, VII. TRUE IDEA OF CREATION.
,, VIII. CREATION SUBJECTED TO VANITY.

CHAPTER I.

APOSTOLIC DEFINITION.

IT is evident that for the investigation of the question which it is proposed to discuss,—viz., "*Does Science aid Faith in regard to Creation?*"—or, to state it more fully, "How is the Christian Faith on the subject of Creation affected by the progress of Science?"—the very first and most essential point to be determined is, "What is the Christian Faith on this subject?" And this we must examine with much care, for it is more than possible that many of the difficulties have arisen from errors or defects in regard to this fundamental question. And by the Christian Faith is meant, that which is derived from Holy Scripture, and is taught and received as such in the Church of Christ.

The first article of this Faith, as set forth in what is called the Apostles' Creed, as containing those fundamental truths which were taught by the Apostles of Christ, is expressed in the words, "*I believe in God the Father Almighty, Maker of Heaven and Earth.*" The general truth, indeed, that Creation is the work of Almighty God, is one that belongs not less to what we understand by Natural Religion than to that which is derived from Revelation. This we must conclude from the teaching of the Apostles themselves. Thus St. Paul and Barnabas, when protesting against the idolatrous worship offered to them by the heathens at Lystra, appealed to their own consciousness that worship was due only to "the living God, who made the heaven and the earth and the sea and all that in them is;" and "Who left not Himself without witness, in that He did good, and gave you from heaven rains and fruitful seasons, filling your hearts with food and gladness."* St. Paul, again, when addressing the Athenians, assumed † as a truth self-evident to their own consciences, that there is a God "that made the world,"—τὸν κόσμον, which included not the earth only, but the whole universe and the heavenly bodies,—"and all things therein;" and Who, as Creator, is "Lord of heaven and earth," and "giveth to all life and breath and all things;" in whom "we live and move and have our being," as even their own poets testified when they said, "For we are also His offspring." And this is the more remarkable when we consider that among his hearers were "Epicurean philosophers," whose philosophy was, or at least was accounted to be, opposed to the religious view of Creation. And yet the apostle took for granted that the religious consciousness of all on this subject was so strong, that he might appeal to it without hesitation as contradicting all such atheistical speculations. Indeed, in his epistle to the Romans,‡ when describing in the first chapter the condition of the heathen world without Revelation, he declares that their sin consisted in "*holding down* the truth in unrighteousness; because that which may be known of God is manifest in them; for God manifested it unto them." And he explains how, in their inner consciousness, God made certain truths as to Himself manifest to them. "For the invisible things of Him since the creation of the world are clearly seen, being perceived through the things that are made, even His everlasting power and divinity: so that they are without excuse."

* Acts xiv. 15-17.   † Acts xvii. 24-29.   ‡ Rom. i. 18-21.

And he proceeds to show what would have been the moral effects of this belief in Almighty God as the Creator, had not their knowledge of this truth been suppressed and overlaid and almost lost through their own love of evil. So that it is evident that belief in God, as the Maker of heaven and earth, is the first and most fundamental principle in all religion; and so necessary to man, that, before that Revelation was given by which man should obtain the full knowledge of God, which is life eternal, this truth was clearly manifested, to all whose hearts were willing to recognise it, in the works of God themselves.

But the Christian Faith as to Creation, as taught in Holy Scripture, and particularly by the apostles of Christ, although its elementary truth was made known to man independently of Revelation, is not only more defined and more developed, so as to enter much more largely and with more moral and spiritual force into the religious life; but is also related to other fundamental verities of that Gospel which is the power of God to man's salvation. And although, in the Old Testament, enough was revealed on this subject of Creation to suffice for that imperfect and preparatory Revelation of God; it is undoubtedly to the New Testament that we must look for the exact definition and the complete exposition of the Faith which the Church of Christ receives and teaches.

In the Epistle to the Hebrews, which, whether it was written by St. Paul himself or by some other apostolic teacher, is accepted by the Church as one of those scriptures from which the Christian Faith is derived, there is given a series of illustrative instances, taken from the Old Testament, of that faith by which God's servants in all ages have been distinguished, and which connects the saints of the Old Testament, ever since the creation, with us who believe in Christ under the gospel. And this series is prefaced by a definition* of the faith on the subject of Creation, so far as that faith is common to us and to the patriarchs. We must therefore regard it as the apostolic interpretation of that Revelation which was given to the fathers, as to this primary truth of all religion, that God is Maker of heaven and earth. Indeed, from the fact of the instances † of Abel and Enoch and Noah, which are recorded in the fourth, and fifth, and subsequent chapters of Genesis, following this reference to Creation, there can be no doubt whatever that the writer had in his mind, when describing the faith on this subject that was common to all the true servants of God, that sacred history of Creation with which the First Book of the Old Law commences. And it is of the utmost importance, therefore, that we should compare this statement of the faith as to Creation—which is derived from that part of the Old Testament, and expounded by apostolic authority—with the history itself to which it refers. For the one will undoubtedly explain the other. In Genesis we find that the account of Creation is prefaced by the words, "In the beginning God created the heaven and the earth." The first act in the process of bringing order and being out of the primary state of formless, indefinite darkness and emptiness, was the command of God, "Let there be light: and there was light." The light and the darkness are separated; and the light, unlike the perpetual glory of God's presence, is intermitting; and from the dawning of the light to the return of the darkness is one Day of God's Creation. Again God uttered His Word, and a second separation, that of the waters below from those above, was made by the firmament of heaven: and this was the second Day of Creation. A third time that Word is uttered, and the dry land and the sea are separated; and as that Divine

* Heb. xi. 3. † Heb. xi. 4-7.

Apostolic Definition.

Word commanded the earth to bring forth the various forms of vegetable life capable of propagating themselves by seed, so it was. And this was the third Day of God's creating work. On the fourth, the same Word of God called into existence lights in the firmament to divide between the day and the night; from which it is evident that the Days of God's Creation—whatever they may mean—are altogether different from these days that mark the time for man. On the fifth Day the Word of God calls forth from the waters all living creatures that are in the seas, and the fowl that fly above the earth in the firmament of heaven. And, lastly, on the sixth Day, the same Word commands the earth to bring forth all the beasts of the earth after their kind, and cattle after their kind, and creeping things after their kind. But here, as the great work approaches its consummation, and the crowning result of Creation is to appear in one who is to be related to God as no other created existence can be, there is a corresponding change in the operation of the Divine Word. It is no longer, as before, God said, "Let man be brought forth, and man was created;" but, "*God said, Let us make man in our image, after our likeness, and let them have dominion over*" the rest of created beings on the earth. "*So God created man in His own image.*"

Such is the history of Creation, of which the apostle gives the summary in these few but very comprehensive words : Πίστει νοοῦμεν κατηρτίσθαι τοὺς αἰῶνας ῥήματι Θεοῦ, εἰς τὸ μὴ ἐκ φαινομένων τὸ βλεπόμενον γεγονέναι; or, as the words may be literally rendered, "*By faith we know that the ages were completely furnished by the Word of God, so that not from things that appear has that which is seen been made.*" The word "*know*" is certainly preferable to "*understand*," which implies a different kind of knowledge from that by which we apprehend the unseen and unthinkable objects of faith.

And it must be observed that here the knowledge is not that which man without Revelation (as St. Paul teaches) can obtain through the works of God, but that which is communicated to us by believing the testimony of God Himself in Holy Scripture. And the knowledge thus acquired has several additional elements beyond that which could be obtained from Nature. First, the work of Creation is described in the terms κατηρτίσθαι τοὺς αἰῶνας. There is no English word that exactly conveys the force of the verb here.* It expresses elsewhere in the New Testament, as well as in classical writers, the act of "bringing into order," "completing an arrangement," "furnishing thoroughly;" and means evidently, when it is compared with the account in Genesis, the work of ordering, or calling existences into their due form and condition—such as is there described as the result of the utterances of God's Word on the successive Days of Creation. Again, it is impossible, when we follow out this comparison, not to understand the αἰῶνας of the writer in the Hebrews as corresponding to the Days of Creation in Genesis. There are, in that chapter, no "*worlds*" besides the earth which are described as being "*furnished;*" even if the word could ever mean, as κόσμος does, the world in its relation to space, which is more than doubtful. The original idea of αἰών is, "time as the condition under which all created things exist, and the measure of their existence." "Thus signifying time, it comes presently to signify all which exists in the world under conditions of time."† So that the αἰῶνας of the apostle in this

---

* In Latin it might be rendered with sufficient exactness by the words *instructa esse sæcula*. The Vulgate has *aptata esse*.

† Trench's "New Testament Synonyms," p. 206. So Alford yet more fully; and he admits this to be the meaning, both in Heb. i. 2 and xi. 3, which Trench doubts.

passage would include both the periods of Time, which itself began to have existence with Creation, and also the creations belonging to each period. And in this sense we must also understand the word in Heb. i. 2, where it is said that the Son of God is He "*by whom He made the aeons.*"

What is signified by these rhythmical successions of Darkness and Light, in regard to the workings of God's creative power, which are called Days in Genesis, and *aeons* by the apostle, is probably at present beyond our power to understand; but at all events the literal interpretation of the word "Day" in Genesis would involve obvious contradictions in the narrative. And when we pass from the six days of God's creation to the seventh day of God's rest, the impossibility of the days of which the inspired record speaks being those which man on earth calls days, is even more obvious. It has been often noticed by commentators in different ages of the Church, that of the seventh day it is not said that the evening and the morning were the seventh day. "God's rest," St. Augustine has said, "is everlasting, without beginning and without end." And so, in later days, Bengel, in commenting on the language of Genesis as to the seventh day, which in the fourth chapter of the Hebrews is made the basis of an argument by the apostle, says of it, "*Deus se quasi in suam recepit tranquillitatem.*" In this chapter of the Epistle to the Hebrews, the apostle reminds those who were familiar with the teaching of the Old Testament, that the rest of God, of which the Law speaks as succeeding, on the seventh day, to the six days of creative action, is the very rest which is promised to all that believe; of which the rest of the Israelites in the land into which Joshua brought them was a figure; of which David speaks in the Psalms as yet future; into which we must labour to enter through faith; for the enjoyment of that rest is reserved for the people of God when they shall have ceased from their earthly labours. From this argument we must conclude, that the seventh day of God's rest which followed the six days of His work of creation is not yet completed.* And if the seventh day is an "aeon," it would be absurd to suppose the previous six days to be such as man's little days of twenty-four hours. We may well say, as Augustine does of other language of this inspired history of Creation: "Here certainly any one, however slow of understanding, ought to wake up to comprehend what kind of days these are which are reckoned."† However, we must examine fully the views of St. Augustine on this subject in a following chapter.

But in the New Testament there is another development of the Faith in regard to Creation, which, although not expressed in the definition we have been considering,—this being of the faith received from the beginning, and common to God's saints of all ages,—is yet implicitly included. For nothing is more distinctly marked, both in the primæval history of the Book of Genesis, and in the summary of it given by the apostle,—nothing more clearly distinguishes the account given in Revelation from that which, as St. Paul teaches, the Gentiles themselves might perceive as to the power and divinity of the Creator in His works,—than the truth that whatever was done was effected by the utterance of the Word of God. But it remained for the Gospel to expound the spiritual meaning of this language in the Revelation of the Son, Who is the *Word* of God. And in man, in relation to whom the whole description of God's work is given, the Greek word λόγος sometimes means language

---

* I quote from a treatise on "The Leading Principles of the Divine Law as Manifested in the Pentateuch," written by me as an Introduction to the Pentateuch in the *Pulpit Commentary*.

† See Note A, in Appendix.

formed in the mind before it is uttered, and is therefore often identified with *Reason*, from which language proceeds; while *Rhema* (ῥῆμα) is speech expressed and uttered, in order to communicate to others the ideas which Reason has conceived. So that when the author of the primæval record in Genesis speaks of all creation as the result of the Divine commands; and when the apostle in the Epistle to the Hebrews says that we learn by faith κατηρτίσθαι τοὺς αἰῶνας ῥήματι Θεοῦ; this implies that there must be a λόγος Θεοῦ from which the uttered word proceeds. Thus much indeed was taught explicitly in the Old Testament, when (in the Book of Proverbs)* Wisdom says: "The Lord possessed me in the beginning of His way, before His works of old. I was set up from everlasting, from the beginning, or ever the earth was." Both before Creation began and when it was effected, "then," Wisdom says, "I was with Him as one brought up with Him." But not until the Gospel came was it revealed that this "Logos," Who was in the beginning with God, and was God; by Whom all things were made, and without Him was not anything made that hath been made; Himself became flesh and dwelt among us, full of grace and truth.

How this revelation of the Logos affects our Faith on the subject of Creation, and how it exhibits the relation of that Faith to human science, will be a subject for our future enquiry. At present, I would only observe that the fact in itself, of the symbolic language of the Book of Genesis having received this exposition and interpretation in the Christian Faith as to the Person of our Lord Jesus Christ, is sufficient to remind us of one principle, perhaps of all the most essential to a right understanding of the history of Creation in the Old Testament. It teaches us emphatically

* Prov. viii. 22-31.

that in this history, given by the Holy Spirit for our instruction and direction,—the history (we must remember) of a Divine work, which preceded the very existence of all human thought, and which it was and is impossible to represent to the mind of man *as it actually was*, under any of our forms of thought; we must of necessity, if we would derive from it the instruction intended, look beyond the mere letter to the spiritual meaning of the language; from the symbol to the thing signified. We must not be led astray by it to form conclusions which are not really the teaching of Holy Scripture itself, but only the erroneous conceptions of our own unspiritual and ignorant minds, which are apt to conceive of God and His divine operations as if He were a man like ourselves. Those who insist on the literal interpretation would themselves hardly imagine that when it is written that "God said, Let there be light," God must be supposed to have spoken as man speaks. If any should conclude from such language as "the right hand" or "the eye" of God, that the Almighty Father must be thought of as in a human form; or if it should be inferred from the expression that "it repented the Lord that He had made man on the earth, and it grieved Him at His heart," that God is not eternal, and omniscient as to the future as well as the present; or that He is subject to human imperfections and passions; we certainly should not consider such literal interpretations to be either rational or reverent. The New Testament expounds to us how, in the case of Creation, one such anthropomorphic expression, "God said," is most significant symbolic language, connected with one of the profoundest mysteries of the Being of God, and that one of the deepest spiritual interest to us men. We may therefore reasonably suppose that in other similar cases, there is some truth, to our mind passing knowledge,—one perhaps which though as yet we know it not, we may know hereafter even in this life through the teaching of Christ's spirit, —but which is concealed from our carnal minds by the symbolic language, even as our Lord's teaching was concealed from the Jews by His parables. At all events, we must not imagine that we are really learning the Mind of God in His Revelation of Himself as the Creator, when we rest in the letter as if it were sufficient, and refuse to understand it in accordance with that which we learn elsewhere of His Infinite Wisdom and Divine Perfections; whether we learn it from the Holy Scriptures themselves or from that which His own works, as St. Paul reminds us, make manifest of Him to those whose hearts are willing to receive their teachings.

But the final clause of this apostolic definition of the Faith as regards Creation is, in one respect, the most significant of all. Commentators are divided as to whether the εἰς τὸ in the original is ecbatic, that is, expresses a *result;* or telic, that is, expresses a *purpose;* for it is capable of either meaning, though the latter is the primary sense from which the other follows. But may we not say it includes both senses? So far as our own knowledge is concerned, it points to the conclusion which follows from our knowing that it was by the Word of God that the perfect work was completed from age to age; and therefore the translation given both in the Authorized and the Revised Version is sufficient. Yet the Greek preposition, which in its ordinary use implies a purpose, may at least remind us that the very end of the Revelation, in the inspired record, of the ages being thoroughly furnished *by the Word of God*, is that we may know, that it was not from the phenomena of nature itself that the visible universe either derived its existence, or received its form, but from God. That Revelation was not made in order to inform us of the processes through which creation was effected, but that we might know that by God's Word the whole was effected; and the order of the development is given in detail in order to teach us how all-powerful and how universally effective that Word is. That the apostle does not intend to deny, that in the processes of creation subordinate means were called into operation by God's Word, is evident from the history itself. The Divine Word commands *the earth* to bring forth the grass of the field and the herb yielding seed, and fruit trees after their kinds; and *the water* to bring forth its inhabitants, and the birds of heaven; and *the earth again* to produce living creatures on the earth; and in accordance with that Word, the Lord God formed man of the dust of the ground. Yet this does not hinder but that the whole creation was made by God, was completed by and in the "Logos," even before the subordinate means were called into exercise. And thus* the sacred record speaks of the creation of the heavens and earth as the work of *one day;* and then, as an explanation of this language, adds, "And (He created) every plant of the field *before it was in the earth*, and every herb of the field *before it grew;* for the Lord God had not caused it to rain upon the earth, and there was not a man to till the ground: but there went up a mist from the earth and watered the whole face of the ground." We surely must infer from all such language, that the truth to be concluded from the Revelation of God as Maker of heaven and earth is *not* that He did not employ subordinate causes for the fulfilment of His work,—the very contrary to this is plainly declared,—but that the origin of all and the effective energy by which all causes acted, was His command, proceeding, as the Christian Faith teaches, from His *Logos* who in the beginning was with God and was and is God.

* Gen. ii. 4-6.

CHAPTER II.

HISTORY OF CREATION NOT SCIENTIFIC.

IN order to discuss the question proposed in this treatise, it has been necessary first of all to examine with some care what that Faith is which is briefly expressed in the first article of the Apostles' Creed. And we have found that this belief as derived from Revelation, and defined and expounded in apostolic teaching, is that it was the power of God's Word acting through the ages necessary for this great work, which both began and completed it; and that whatever physical causes might be employed in its accomplishment, yet that God alone, by His Word, was both the Author and Finisher of Creation.

This faith is the very first element in all true religion; and the more definite and complete the belief is, the more powerful is the influence that it exercises in the religious life. The Law given of old by God to His chosen people begins with the Revelation of God as Creator. The praises of Him whose glory, power, wisdom, and goodness are manifest in the works of His Creation are the theme of psalmists and prophets. Even in heaven the most exalted intelligences are represented as casting their crowns before the throne of God, and saying,* "Worthy art Thou to receive the glory and the honour and the power; for Thou

* Rev. iv. 11.

didst create all things, and because of Thy Will they were, and were created." While on earth the confidence of God's servants in Him as able to relieve and help has always been founded on the belief that He is the Creator: "Happy is He whose hope is in the Lord his God, which made heaven and earth, the sea, and all that therein is;"* "My help cometh from the Lord, who made heaven and earth."† And yet further, the Revelation in the New Testament of the Redemption of Man has its foundation in the relations of man to God as his Creator. The whole of Religion, regarded as including our duty to God and man, rests on the truths which the history of Creation teaches, that man is made in the image and likeness of God, and is God's representative on the earth. In fact, take away from the Bible the first chapter of Genesis, and the basis of all the subsequent revelation of God to man is gone.

But while this Revelation of God as "the Maker of heaven and earth" is of such incalculable value to our moral and spiritual life, there are some points that must be considered in order to clear away false conceptions of its nature.

1. In the first place, it must be remembered that the Revelation, proceeding, as it does, from the Creator Himself, is yet made *to* man, *for* man's spiritual benefit, and *through* man; for whether Moses himself was the writer, or this was a primitive record embodied by him in the Book of the Law, it was communicated undoubtedly through the agency of the human mind. We must therefore expect that the standpoint of the description of God's work in Creation would be the earth that man inhabits, which was made by God as the scene in which man should be placed to serve and glorify his Creator, and in which those marvels of

---

* Psalm cxlvi. 5-6. † Psalm cxxi. 2.

Redeeming Love in the Incarnation, the Passion, and the Resurrection of the Son of God were to be manifested, which would as far exceed the marvels of Creating Power, as things spiritual surpass things material, and eternity surpasses time. The language, therefore, in which the Revelation is made is the language of the children of men. It is this world and all that pertains to it, and not the rest of the universe, except so far as it affects human life, of which the history speaks. The light and darkness are those which man knows as the light of the day and the darkness of the night. The firmament is the sky above our heads, which seems to separate the waters above which descend on the earth in showers and floods, from those which are below. The dry land which appears is the earth with its continents and islands; the waters gathered together are the seas. The lights in the firmament are the sun and moon, made to divide day and night, and for signs and for seasons, and for days and years; purposes all belonging to human life and to all its necessities and requirements. The stars are only mentioned incidentally as contributing to the same ends. And so, throughout, everything is described in its relation to human life, and as it is known and perceived by the senses of man. For the purpose of the Revelation is neither to satisfy man's curiosity as to worlds unknown, nor yet to give him that knowledge which his own reason may itself obtain by patient and accurate observation of the things of nature; but to impress upon him the truth, that all things around him, all things which affect his life on earth, are from God. He must recognize God in all nature, as the Creator from whom it has proceeded. And not only is this the one purpose for which the Revelation is given, but we can easily perceive very sufficient reason why it should not form any part of that purpose to communicate such knowledge of natural things as man's own natural faculties, if sufficiently cultivated, can themselves acquire. For a revelation of that kind of truth which we understand by scientific truth, far from being a benefit to man, would have been, on the whole, a serious injury; for if that truth were learnt from Divine authority instead of requiring patient, continued, and accurate research, it would have impeded instead of encouraged the cultivation of man's intellect. While, on the other hand, the Revelation, being given in such a form as speaks directly to the senses of man, is best suited to bring the truth it reveals as to our Creator directly home to the mind of every man in all the circumstances of his earthly life.

2. But there is more to be considered in respect of the nature of this revelation of God as "Maker of heaven and earth." It is, we see, valuable to us, not as giving to us the kind of information that science supplies to man, but, we may almost say, because it does not supply such knowledge. But further, the purpose of the Revelation being totally different from that of science, the attempt to make the inspired history of Creation fit in with the scientific view may be expected to fail, for several very sufficient reasons. First of all, science deals with the phenomena of the visible universe; its aim is to distinguish them accurately, to classify them so as best to exhibit both the order and the unity of nature; to determine the succession of phenomena, and explain such succession, so far as it is able, as a necessary sequence of cause and effect; or if this cannot be done, as a phenomenal law, true so far as our observation and experience can reach. But when Revelation speaks of the work of God in Creation, and teaches us to regard the whole visible universe as the result, not of the phenomena of nature, but of the operation of God's Word and God's Spirit, it speaks of original causes and effects, lying wholly beyond

History of Creation not Scientific. 27

human knowledge, and it cannot represent them to us *except in their results*, which are the objects of our senses. And there is a further reason, which is apt to be entirely overlooked by those who acquire a superficial knowledge of scientific conclusions, without having thought much as to the foundations of physical science; indeed one which seems never to have been sufficiently considered in reference to this subject. And this is, that the inspired history of the creation of heaven and earth could not (we may say with all reverence) have used the language of physical science to describe the work of creation, because *this language is not the truth*. If any one is disposed to demur to this, let him ask himself what science it is, the language of which is perfectly true, and expresses the whole truth as to nature and its phenomena? Of course it will not be supposed that the ancient science of the Greeks or Chaldeans or Egyptians, or mediæval science, was the whole truth, or indeed anything approaching to it; or anything more than hypotheses more or less probable, none of which could be verified, and most of which are now known to be untrue. But is not modern science, which tests its hypotheses through careful and exhaustive processes of induction, able to use language which is the truth? Those who can suppose this must understand very little what physical science means. Such science, to be of any value at all, must be always progressive; it is ever pressing onwards towards a goal *which to the mind of man is always unattainable*. But even some who are accounted philosophers seem but partially to apprehend this truth. "In the writings of some recent philosophers, especially Auguste Comte, and in some degree John Stuart Mill," the late Professor Jevons observes in his " Principles of Science,"* " there is an erro-

* Vol. ii., p. 448.

neous and hurtful tendency to represent our knowledge as assuming an approximately complete character. At least these and many other writers fail to impress upon their readers a truth, which I think cannot be too constantly borne in mind, namely, that the utmost successes which our scientific method can accomplish will not enable us to comprehend more than an infinitesimal fraction of what there is doubtless to comprehend." Nor is it even true, as some state it, that although we can never in our knowledge bring natural phenomena completely under mathematical laws, yet the progress of our sciences may ever be converging towards completeness. "On the contrary, it appears to me," Jevons observes, "the supply of new and unexplained facts is *divergent* in extent, so that the more we have explained the more there is to explain." "In whatever direction we extend our investigations and successfully harmonize a few facts, the result is only to raise up a host of other unexplained facts. Can any scientific man venture to state that there is less opening now for new discoveries than there was three centuries ago? Is it not rather true that we have but to open a scientific book, and read a page or two, and we shall in all probability come to some recorded phenomenon of which no precise explanation can yet be given?"* The fact is, that so many new fields have been opened for future discoveries, and the quickened energies of the human mind are so eagerly pressing onwards in every conceivable direction to larger and more comprehensive views of nature and the visible universe, that the language of Physical Science in the present day is liable to any amount of change.

It is quite possible that in less than fifty years, theories now accepted as primary laws of the universe may be, so

* "Principles of Science," ii., 450-451.

History of Creation not Scientific. 29

to speak, absorbed in other theories far more comprehensive, which may render obsolete our present scientific language as quite unsuitable for the more advanced science of the future. And yet whatever these more complete theories may be, they will only open more questions for investigation. For example, the universal law of gravitation, though known for two centuries, is as yet unexplained. The only theory that appears to scientific men to be any approach towards an explanation would certainly open many more questions for solution than those which it solves. The undulatory theory of light is compelled to assume the existence of an "ether" pervading all space, which though rarer than any vacuum that art could produce, so as to be unaffected to any appreciable extent by the force of gravity, yet has some of the properties of a solid. This theory, even if altogether true as a mechanical hypothesis, can only be considered at present as the first step towards the solution of the infinitely larger question of the relations of light, heat, electricity, magnetism, and chemical activity. The very constitution of matter is an unsolved mystery. The atomic theory, in its latest form of the whole visible universe being composed of rotating rings of the ether, leaves untouched the further question, what is the constitution of the ethereal medium. Is that composed of separate indivisible molecules, or is it a continuous substance? Difficulties apparently insuperable present themselves against either view. In fact, examine all such subjects below the surface of the provisional scientific hypothesis, and the conclusion must inevitably force itself upon our mind, that science is not only unable in its present state of progress to use language which is the truth, but that there is no reason whatever to suppose that it could ever become capable of doing this. "It is the mere pedantry of science to condemn as untrue popular language, the language of the senses; as if those things which science regards as realities were anything else than effects of yet higher causes, such as doubtless would be found, could we comprehend them, to differ as widely from the conceptions of science, as these do from our immediate perceptions of the phenomena." *

Let us take one instance in the history of Creation to illustrate how dangerous it may be to attempt to make the conclusions of science fit in with the language of Revelation in regard to creation. The first creating act there described is that which called light into existence. The sublimity of the sentence, " God said, Let light be, and light was," which made Longinus acknowledge that the writer was no ordinary man, consists in *light* being the subject. If we should substitute for it *heat*, or *energy*, or *the ether*, or any physical cause, there is no sublimity whatever in the sentence. It was the *result* that followed God's word, through what intermediate causes signifies not, that *was the creation*. "God," St. Paul says,† " that commanded light to shine out of darkness, hath shined in our hearts." And we need no scientific knowledge to inform us why *light* was the first work in the creation of the visible universe; why when that which was being brought into its existence and its form was τὸ βλεπόμενον, that, by which it could be seen and distinguished, was first of all to be called into existence. And it is quite sufficient to know that this followed the command of God, without enquiring what the physical cause of light may be. It seems to be imagined that the discovery of the theory that light is the effect of the undula-

---

* "On the True Relations of Scientific Thought and Religious Belief" (Paper read before the Victoria Institute, by the Bishop of Edinburgh), p. 5.

† 2 Cor. iv. 6.

History of Creation not Scientific. 31

tion of an all-pervading ether was necessary to the belief that it was called into existence before the lights in the firmament of heaven were created. As if man could not conceive, and did not actually know, before all theories as to the nature of light, that in the flash from the clouds of heaven, and in the flames of the fire that devoured the forests, there was light independent both of the sun by day and of the moon by night.

In former days, indeed, it seemed an easy objection to the history of Creation, that light was created before the sun and moon and stars. Then the tables seemed to be turned when science taught that light had an existence in the universe distinct from all these ordinary sources of light. In the present day one might be strongly tempted to reply to the objections of scientists to the inspired history, You see after all that Scripture has understood more of the true constitution of the universe than your science had found out till the present day. The very first creation of God, science now discovers, must have been that which the Bible declares it was. Not only is that medium which produces light also that which conveys *heat*, the universal form of *energy* throughout the visible universe; but, in fact, according to the theory most approved by the first mathematicians of modern times, it is the very material of which this universe is composed; each atom being a rotating ring of the ether itself. Such a reply might perhaps seem to be the true answer to give to the objections of scientists, and not only sufficient but conclusive; a complete victory for Faith gained by the aid of Science. But, in my judgment, it would be to repel for the time one erroneous idea as to the teaching of Scripture, by another no less serious. It can only lead to confusion of thought, and of faith itself, if we suppose the history of Creation to require human science to explain its teaching.

Our theories may be very convenient hypotheses to explain (for example) the phenomena of light and heat, and to determine their connection and succession. But to bring these theories into our interpretation of the revelation of God's work in creation is, on the one hand, to degrade the simple majesty of the Word of God, when we make its meaning to be that of utterly defective theories which man's reason frames as aids for its further investigations; while on the other hand it exposes God's truth to contempt, in the case of these theories giving way to others more comprehensive and profound, which may not so readily lend themselves to our attempts to mix up together two things that are *incommensurable;* that is, the finite knowledge of human science, and the infinite knowledge of Divine wisdom.*

* See Note B in Appendix.

CHAPTER III.

GOD'S GLORY IN CREATION.

THE first act of God's creating work, in which light was brought out of darkness through His Word, is an instance (we have seen) of the necessity of regarding the history of Creation simply as the record of the results effected by the Creating Word, and not confusing and obscuring that Divine record by any theories—however plausible or provisionally to be accepted as true,—by which science may explain the process through which they were effected. But the significance of the Creation of Light, in relation to the whole of the six days' work, consummated and perfected, as it is, in the creation of man, is far too important to be dismissed without further examination. Light holds a position in the physical universe which belongs to nothing else that is merely physical; and it is the more necessary to discuss this fully, because it brings us into a sphere of thought, which human reason cannot fail to recognise as real, and yet as not only transcending the range of the theories of physical science, but as being, in some aspects of its relations to man, beyond the scope of its best established conclusions.

The relation of light to the whole visible creation as τὸ βλεπόμενον has been already noticed, and is sufficiently obvious. But it must be observed also, that whatever relation light may have, from its chemical or other action, with inorganic matter or vegetable life, it is only with animal life, and above all with rational life, that it has any relation as being light, that which manifests. And in the physical world, as well as in the spiritual,* it is literally and strictly true, not merely that "*whatsoever doth make manifest*," but also "*everything that is made manifest, is light.*" The explanation of the manifestation of the external universe to man, and indeed all animal life,—an explanation which depends on no theory of the physical nature of light, or the mode of its transmission,—is that objects, not themselves luminous, are manifested by the light that falls on them being itself modified by the form, and character, and surface of these objects, and being thence reflected in all directions so as to produce sensations in the eye corresponding to the objects. Light is created for the eye, and the eye is created for light. "*The lamp of the body is the eye.*"† This organ, as an optical instrument by means of which an image on the retina is produced, is constructed on principles which human science can both explain and follow in practical art; but as an organ of vision, by which cognition of the object is obtained through the sensations produced by this image on the nerves of the retina, science is not only incapable of giving the full explanation, but never can give any real explanation whatever. It is "unthinkable," as all nature is, when we look the least below its surface.

This conclusion, namely *that Light is the medium of communication between Creation and Reason*, while it is expounded to us by science, is, as I have said, independent of all scientific hypotheses as to the physical nature of light, although it is consistent with that theory which science

* Ephes. v. 13, πᾶν τὸ φανερούμενον φῶς ἐστι.
† St. Matt. vi. 22.

God's Glory in Creation. 35

accepts in the present day, at all events as provisionally true. And what pre-eminence in Creation does this one conclusion give to light! It must be observed that nothing else in nature, however nearly related to light mechanically, whether in the subtle mechanism of the ether, or otherwise,—such as heat, electricity, magnetism, chemical action, etc.,—however important a part any of them may play in the physical constitution and energies of the material universe, holds or can hold the same relation to intelligence of any kind that light holds. It is not without sufficient cause that Christian thought has always regarded the creation of light on the first day of the creation of the physical universe, as symbolical and a very representative of the revelation of that spiritual light by which man has the knowledge of God, which is in him life eternal. Indeed, in the subsequent religious history of mankind, in which, by God's primæval ordinance, human life has been divided into weeks of solar days, answering to the six Days (or æons) of God's creation followed by a Day of the rest of God,— while, until the redemption of man by Christ, the seventh day of the week was selected as the most appropriate for the religious worship of that economy;—the first day was that on which the revelation of the light of the Gospel was made by the resurrection of the incarnate Son of God from the dead; and on that day also, the Holy Ghost was given to complete that revelation as the Spirit of life and energy and truth. Henceforth, the first day, the day of light, *Dies solis*, was the day of worship for the Church of Christ, and was entitled the Lord's Day.* And when the final revelation of Jesus Christ, which God gave Him, was made

---

* Rev. i. 10. See instances given in Alford's note of the frequent use of the words "dominica" and κυριακή, in this application by primitive Christian writers.

through the favoured apostle, in order to supply His Universal Church with such knowledge of the things that should come to pass until His second coming in glory, as should guide them in the bodily absence of Him who is the Light,—again, this revelation was made on the first day. "*I was in the Spirit,*" St. John says, "*on the Lord's day.*"

And further we must observe, that, no doubt in accordance with this—I mean, *that Light is related to Reason* as nothing else in creation is, being the direct and immediate cause of the cognition of created things by reason,—Holy Scripture, both in the Old Testament and in the New, speaks of light as that creature of God, which of all things not endued with life and with reason has the nearest affinity with His own being. "Thou coverest Thyself," the Psalmist says,* "with light as with a garment." "He only hath immortality dwelling in light unapproachable," St. Paul teaches.† And the Apostle John says more expressly,‡ "This is the message which we have heard from Him, and announce unto you, that God is light, and in Him is no darkness at all." And, further, whenever there has been, either under the Law or under the Gospel, any visible manifestation of Divine Majesty, light, sometimes too bright for human vision to bear, is the symbol and representation of the glory of God. When our Lord Himself was transfigured in the mount in the presence of His disciples, to reveal to them by anticipation some of the glory of His future kingdom, "His face shone as the sun, and His garments became white as the light."§ And when the apostle St. John saw the vision of the Son of Man in the midst of the Churches, the Sovereign and High Priest of the Kingdom of Heaven,

---

* Psalm civ. 2. † 1 Tim. vi. 16.
‡ 1 John i. 5. § Matt. xviii. 2.

"His countenance was as the sun shineth in his strength."* In fact, we are so familiar with this kind of representation of heavenly and Divine glory, and it seems so natural and appropriate, that perhaps it has never occurred to us to ask ourselves what is the meaning that underlies such symbolical language, or representation.

But, in the pre-eminence given to light in the sacred history of Creation, that which specially concerns our argument in this treatise is, that it presents nature to us, not simply or primarily as a work contrived for purposes necessary or useful, but first of all as a *spectacle* in which the glory of God is manifested by that light which is the most suitable symbol of the spiritual light that surrounds the throne of Him who is invisible. God reveals in Creation first and above all His *glory;* as the seraphims above the Divine throne, which the prophet Isaiah saw in vision, proclaimed in responsive chorus, "Holy, holy, holy, is the Lord God of Hosts; *the whole earth is full of His glory.*"†

By the creation of light, nature is visible to animal life, by all endued with that which is implied by the Greek word ψυχὴ, for all the purposes necessary to that life; while in man it also speaks to his logical faculty, or what is called νοῦς,—by which, through "discourse of reason" or science, he can recognise in nature sequences of cause and effect, and can derive from them proofs of the wisdom and power of the Creator, and thus he can conclude design. But in man, beyond and above all these, it speaks to a higher faculty, his spirit or πνεῦμα, in which his likeness to his Creator most of all consists. And this enables man to behold in nature the glory of God; and to all whose spirit is purified from earthly and carnal feeling, and quickened into its true life, this is a far more distinct and immediate wit-

* Rev. i. 16. † Isa. vi. 3.

ness to the presence of God in His creation than any that can be supplied by the lower faculties of his being. The sense of beauty and glory of creation is an effect on the mind wholly independent, both of the use of nature to the animal life, and of the conclusions that science may draw as to the constitution of nature; it arises immediately from the view of nature simply as τὸ βλεπόμενον, when seen by one capable of fully recognizing that which he beholds. Professor Mozley, in his profoundly interesting discussion of this subject in his sermon on Nature, says of this, "The glory of nature in reality resides in the mind of man; there is an inward intervening light through which the material objects pass, a transforming medium which converts the physical assemblage into a picture." This is no doubt true, in the sense in which Professor Mozley used these words, of such objects of sight as that of which he was speaking, namely, the glory of a landscape; the special beauty of which depends chiefly on the arrangement and disposition of the natural objects. But it may be questioned by some whether it is equally true of the beauty of separate objects in nature, as, for example, of a beautiful flower. We must analyze the process that takes place in vision in order to state the truth somewhat more accurately than Mozley has done. That which reaches the eye is, of course, not the material object itself, but the light coming from it, which forms an image on the retina, which the ψυχή even of an animal transfers to the object itself from which the light has proceeded. This is the case both as regards form and colour. As regards the latter, it is indeed very difficult for one not scientifically taught, not to believe that the colour is in the object itself, whereas it is certain that it is the light that reaches the eye that produces the sensation of colours; indeed, the present conclusion of science is that as *colour* it has merely a subjective existence, and is due to the triple constitution of nerves within the eye. It is evident then that, as has been before observed, the cognition of the object, whether such cognition as an animal may have, or such as the intelligence of man obtains of it as a subject for reason, or such as the higher faculty has of it as beautiful and glorious, is due, *in all cases*, whether in animal or in man, to the light that the eye receives. But in each case the inner faculty *interprets* the sensations produced by the light; only there is this difference between the several cases referred to. In the two former,* the relation of the object to animal life in regard to its use for food, or the danger it threatens, and the like, would be the same whether it were visible or not. And in man's own vision, that character of the object which science can investigate would be unaltered by its being unseen; whereas the beauty and glory of it is entirely the result of its being seen, and do not exist except in the mind that is capable of recognizing such characters in it.† Yet it is not true, as Professor Mozley's words might be misunderstood to mean, that the beauty and glory are the mere creation of the human mind itself; but they must have (to use the language of Aristotle with regard to all external nature) first of all a *potential existence* in the creation of God, in order that the mind that is capable may give them an actual and subjective existence within itself.

We may take a few instances in nature as illustrations which Holy Scripture supplies. Our Lord Himself refers to the "lilies of the field" as clothed by God with a beauty surpassing all the glory of Solomon. One of these, which grows still in great abundance in the rich valleys of

---

* See Mozley's Sermon on Nature, p. 126.
† See Note C. in Appendix.

Palestine, is described* as a flower of great beauty and
dignity. "The three inner petals meet above and form a
gorgeous canopy, such as art never approached, and king
never sat under in all his glory." These flowers are the
favourite food of the wild gazelles; this is the animal view
of that which God has clothed with a beauty excelling all
the art of man. Science again can distinguish its botanical
characters, examine its tissues, expound the processes of
its growth; this is the view of reason,—but what is all this
to its beauty and glory? But the higher faculty in man
sees it first, and above all things, as beautiful; he seeks
to imitate it, and recognizing that beauty as representing to
his mind some of the glory of His Creator, he carves the
graceful forms of the flowers and leaves of the lilies on the
capitals of the columns for the temple of God. Even as
true Christian feeling also, in seasons of joy and praise,
places in our churches flowers of beauty and glory; not as
mere ornaments, but to set forth, by those creations of our
God, the true spiritual beauty of the Lord in His sanctuary.
Indeed the almost Divine significance of the beauty of
nature, as God's work, quite distinct from all ideas of its
usefulness to man and beast, is not unfrequently indicated
in Holy Scripture. How full of spiritual meaning are the
simple words, "The winter is past, the rain is over and
gone, the flowers appear on the earth." And again in those
by which special Divine excellence is intimated, "I am
the rose of Sharon, and the lily of the valleys."† Again,
the beauty of precious stones, although made manifest by
the art of man, is no less truly the creation of God than the
glory of the flowers of the field. The promise given by

* "The Land and the Book," i. 394, quoted in Smith's "Dictionary of
the Bible."
† Cant. ii. 1, 2.

God's Glory in Creation. 41

God to the afflicted and desolate Church of the old Testament was, "I will lay thy stones with fair colours and thy foundations with sapphires, and I will make thy windows of agates, and thy gates of carbuncles, and all thy borders of precious stones. And all thy children shall be taught of the Lord ; and great shall be the peace of thy children."*

It is impossible adequately to express the idea of spiritual light, except through those of natural beauty and glory, which are wholly out of the sphere of the merely logical faculty. Truth itself is not known and distinguished truly, except its beauty is recognized. And therefore in the descriptions of the blessedness of the New Jerusalem which is to come down from heaven, objects of surpassing natural beauty, and not merely those of conventional value, can alone express the spiritual idea. " The city was *pure gold, like unto pure glass.*" And not only are all the twelve foundations laid in precious stones of diverse colours, but "the twelve gates were twelve pearls."† It is impossible not to be reminded of the parable in which our Lord illustrates‡ that spiritual insight into the value of the "kingdom of heaven," which disposes a man to surrender all for its sake, from the conduct of a merchant who is able to recognize the surpassing beauty and therefore the extraordinary value of a single pearl.

Another illustration which Holy Scripture suggests is, in some respects, even more direct and pertinent. "The appearance of the bow in the cloud in the day of rain," as the prophet Ezekiel,§ with almost scientific exactness, describes the rainbow, is the one instance in nature of light not giving beauty to a natural object, but simply revealing its own beauty and glory. With animal life it has no relation

* Isa. lxv. 11-13.   † Rev. xxi. 18-22.
‡ Matt. xiii. 45, 46.   § Ezek. i. 28.

whatever. Science explains it as the effect, to the eye of a spectator, of the light from the sun falling on spherical drops of water, and being reflected internally with great brilliance. But this explanation, though very interesting, is yet exceedingly prosaic; it can tell us nothing at all of that feeling which the bow in the cloud inspires in the heart of man:

> "My heart springs up when I behold
> A rainbow in the sky;
> So was it when my life began;
> So is it now I am a man;
> So be it when I shall grow old,
> Or let me die!"

Without attempting to analyse this sense of its beauty, and thus spoil the purity and reality of that beauty, as a direct revelation of God's glory in His creation, we may yet observe that it consists not merely in the beautiful harmony of the tender bands of the several colours into which the pure white light is separated, but in the dignity and majesty of the noble arch that appears to span the sky and rest upon the earth, and yet more in the contrast between this vision of glory and the dark storm on which it appears. It is a revelation of the beauty of heaven in the midst of the dark clouds of earth. As such, it was selected by God Himself,* as the outward and visible token of the covenant with Noah and all mankind, made after the Flood, that the world should not again be destroyed by water. And in the visions,† both of Ezekiel and of St. John in the Apocalypse, the brightness round about the throne of God, in the midst of which the glory was too intense for the eye of man to rest upon, and from which proceeded thunderings and lightnings, was a rainbow or halo, in which the light shone in softened tints.

* Gen. ix. 12-17. † Ezek. i. 28; Rev. iv. 3.

In such instances as these of the flowers of the field and the rainbow, the Word and Spirit of God themselves direct our thoughts to the beauty which the mind of man recognizes in the Creation of God, through the light which first of all He commanded to shine out of darkness. But I refer to such distinct and definite recognition in Holy Writ, not as if these were some exceptional instances of the relation of natural objects of beauty to Divine ideals, but simply as reminding us, that in all cases it is only by looking through Nature to that which underlies it, to the invisible reality which is Divine and Eternal, and of which Nature is the visible witness, that we can truly appreciate that which is beautiful and glorious therein. It would be a mistake, however, to suppose that this looking through Nature to Divine ideals of beauty and glory, implies that we distinguish these as something, which the understanding presents to us in any defined form of thought. On the contrary, the very power that a spectacle of grandeur or loveliness has to affect the soul, consists chiefly in its being that which can be neither described nor understood; the mind must be passive and silent in its presence, in order that the vision may produce its own effect on our mind, and fill the soul with itself. Few persons have not felt this, when standing, for example, in the presence of Niagara, or of some grand Alpine range clothed in eternal snow; or on one of those delicious mornings which come even in England at the beginning of summer; or on a calm evening at sea in the tropics, when the sun is setting in the midst of clouds tinted with all the hues of the rainbow, and edged with gold;—at such times few are not conscious of a silent joy, which approaches at times to awe, in the contemplation of Nature, such as to attempt to analyze and express would be almost profane. Indeed, wherever this beauty speaks to us, whether in a simple flower of the field, or in the most majestic mountain scenery, it is only such a spirit that can receive its teachings. The soul, when smitten thus by a sublime idea, "feeds on the pure bliss and takes her rest in God."

It is, however, very necessary to remember, as Mozley warns us,* that although the beauty of Nature is as truly a part of God's creation as its material framework is, and, indeed, a far higher and more Divine part,—yet it is "a religious communication only to those who come to it with the religious element already in themselves; no man can get a religion out of the beauty of Nature. There must be for the base of a religion the internal view, the inner sense, the look into ourselves. . . . If there is not this, outward nature cannot of itself enlighten man's conscience, and give him a knowledge of God." In fact, the beauty of creation has been, in all ages to the present hour, as much an incentive to the idolatry of Nature in some form or other, as the beauty of woman, which is also God's creation, has been to fleshly lust. The patriarch Job, in enumerating the temptations to forsake God his Maker, which he had resisted and overcome, lays special emphasis on this; "If I beheld the sun" (literally the *light*) "when it shineth, or the moon walking in brightness; and my heart hath been secretly enticed, or my mouth hath kissed my hand; this also were an iniquity to be punished by the Judge; *for I should have denied the God that is above.*"* Such kind of Atheism, or, as St. Paul calls it, of "worshipping and serving the creature rather than the Creator, Who is blessed for ever," was, it seems, the earliest defection from God. We might almost say that, in a more intellectual and refined form, it is the latest, at least in the poetic mind; in the scientific mind, Nature-worship takes the lower and more unspiritual form, of

* Sermon on Nature, p. 140.   * Job xxxi. 26-28.

the idolatry of physical law. But for both these, the Christian faith on the subject of creation supplies the remedy by teaching that both its beauty and its order are only from God; that in the one we may see His glory, in the other His wisdom. And in the eloquent words of him to whose sermon on Nature I have frequently referred in this chapter, "When men have started from outward nature, when they have used it as a foundation, and made it their first stay, its glory has issued in gloom and despondency; but to those who have first made the knowledge of themselves and their own souls their care, it has ever turned to light and hope. They have read in Nature an augury and a presage; they have found in it a language and a revelation; and they have caught in it signs and intimations of Him, Who has clothed Himself with it as with a garment, Who has robed Himself with its honour and majesty, decked Himself with its light, and Who created it as an expression and manifestation of Himself."*

Or the same truth may be expressed in the language, no less true, though far less profound, of a writer of a very different school of thought. "The mere majesty of God's power and greatness," Dr. Chalmers says, "when offered to your notice, lays hold of one of the faculties within you. The holiness of God, with His righteous claim of legislation, lays hold of another of these faculties. The difference between them is so great that the one may be engrossed and interested to the full, while the other remains untouched, and in a state of entire dormancy. Now, it is no matter what it be that ministers delight to the former of these two faculties. If the latter be not arrested and put on its proper exercise, you are making no approximation whatever to the right habit and character of religion. There are

* Mozley's "University Sermons," p. 144.

a thousand ways in which you may gratify your taste for that which is beauteous and majestic. It may find its gratification in the loveliness of a vale, or in the freer and bolder outlines of an upland situation, or in the terrors of a storm, or in the sublime contemplations of astronomy, or in the magnificent idea of a God who sends forth the wakefulness of His omniscient eye, and the vigour of His upholding hand, throughout all the realms of nature and of providence."*

"The religion of taste is one thing, the religion of conscience is another." A truth, indeed, most necessary to be remembered, and too often forgotten. Yet when conscience is purified from dead works to serve the living and true God, it is no small aid to our faith in the Creator, and our apprehension of His glorious perfections, and therefore an incentive to our praise, that He has left us in the beauty of His works a witness to His glory, no less certain, and even more distinct, than the testimony which they give to His law by their order.

* Chalmers' "Astronomical Discourses," Sermon vii.

CHAPTER IV.

CREATION THE WORK OF WISDOM.

IT has been already observed that the patriarchal faith on the subject of Creation, viz., that it was effected by the spoken Word of God, is in the Christian Faith further developed and expounded by the truth, that the "Logos," who was in the beginning with God, and was God, is He through whose Divine operation all things were made. And we also inferred generally from the term used by St. John to represent the Second Person of the Trinity, implying the word conceived in the mind by reason before it is expressed, that the language of the Old Testament respecting Divine wisdom was an anticipation of the more complete revelation of the New. But we must now examine more fully what is the force and meaning of this part of the Christian Faith as affecting our view of the creating work of God. We have already assumed that, although the Word of God was the one original cause of all the effects produced, we must not therefore conclude that no intermediate and subordinate causes were employed for this end; indeed occasional indications of the interposition of such causes were pointed out. We have now to take a step further and shew that the very truth, that the Word or active Wisdom of God was the agent by which creation was effected, itself implies that subordinate means were used for the fulfilment of the ends.

The idea of God, whether in creation or in any other of His works, which is most natural to the mind of man, and which, if uncorrected by the teaching of revelation,—too often indeed among those who live in the full light of revelation,—seems to absorb all His other attributes, is that of infinite and almighty power. It seems to such persons (and they are many), not only consistent with the perfections of Deity, but even the highest proof of the greatness and majesty of God, that He should work immediately by the mere authority of Sovereign will. The interposition of subordinate means implies, they imagine, limitations of power. This, however, is not the Christian Faith, nor is it the teaching even of the more ancient Revelation, of which that Faith is only the fully-developed form. It is the very purpose of Holy Scripture throughout to reveal God as One in Whom the several perfections of Deity are not merely present as attributes distinct from Himself, but are indivisibly and inseparably united, so that they of necessity combine and co-operate in all Divine works.

Nothing indeed is more frequently declared even in the Old Testament, when the Creation of God is described, than that by His wisdom, no less than by His power, this Divine work was accomplished. "The Lord by wisdom hath founded the earth; by understanding hath He established the Heavens; by His knowledge the depths are broken up, and the clouds drop down the dew."* The Psalmist in that glorious nature psalm to which we shall refer in a following chapter for other aspects of Creation, says of it, "O Lord, how marvellous are Thy works; in wisdom hast Thou made them all."† And the prophet Jeremiah combines the several

* Prov. iii. 19, 20, † Psalm civ.

Creation the Work of Wisdom. 49

Divine attributes, " He hath made the earth by His power ; He hath established the world by His wisdom ; and hath stretched out the Heaven by His understanding."*

Now it must be observed that *wisdom*—with the corresponding words both in Hebrew and in Greek—as compared with other cognate words,—such as those which are rendered "understanding," "knowledge," "prudence," and the like,—whatever other distinctions may be observed amongst them, always expresses the highest and noblest kind of knowledge ; and has been defined as including both the striving after the best and highest ends, as well as the using the best means,† so that "there can be no true wisdom disjoined from goodness." This seems on the whole to be the most complete and exact definition of wisdom ; though it is well defined also by other writers, both Christian and heathen, as the knowledge which includes both those things that are Divine and those that are human, things eternal and temporal ; and also as the reason which has insight into the causes or inner principles of things, as distinguished from the understanding, which apprehends and appreciates their application. Without, however, confining ourselves strictly to any one formal definition, the question of wisdom, both in man and in God Himself, is so fully discussed in the Old Testament Scriptures, and especially with reference to the work of God as Creator, that it will be sufficient for our argument to examine this teaching, as affecting the question of the use of intermediate means in the creation of the visible universe.

There is no book of the Sacred Volume in which the subject is more clearly stated, and the comparison between human wisdom and Divine more distinctly exhibited, than

---

* Jer. li. 15.
† Trench's "Synonyms of the New Testament."

the Book of Job. The questions as to the date of this book, its relation to the Mosaical books, and its character,—whether strictly historical or a sacred poem,—do not concern our argument. Being received, not only by the Jews, to whom were entrusted the oracles of God, but also by the Church of Christ, as part of those Scriptures which are "given by inspiration of God," and therefore the source of our faith, the view which it gives of the Divine wisdom as exercised in the work of Creation must be accepted as of plenary authority in regard to the Christian faith on this subject. The importance of this, in discussing the question of the relation between human science and the Creation of God, will be manifest as we examine it.

It will be observed, by all who study the Book of Job with any attention, that in the twenty-sixth chapter—when his three friends had finished their mistaken condemnation of his conduct—while he allows that he had himself previously misapprehended the providential government of God, and could not even yet understand the cause of his own sufferings,—he was content to accept that which Creation itself taught him as to the wisdom of God transcending, not only in degree, but in its very character, all human understanding. In the twenty-eighth chapter he confesses that all human wisdom, though it may be of much value to man as regards temporal things, yet differs essentially from the wisdom of God. The marvellous faculties with which God has endowed man,—beyond the keen eye of the eagle, or the strength and vigour of the lion,—do indeed enable him not only to subdue the earth and make it fruitful, but to explore its secrets and turn its darkness into light; to penetrate into its depths, to break its rocks in pieces and tunnel its mountains; in fact, to conquer Nature and make it serve his purposes and to enrich himself with its trea-

Creation the Work of Wisdom. 51

sures. And if this was true in the time of the patriarch, how much more is it fulfilled in the present day! Yet, whatever secrets of Nature all this skill and enterprise of practical science may discover, they do not bring man one step nearer wisdom. It is declared by the Atheist that he dissects every fibre, he explores every secret place in Nature, he scrutinizes every cell with his microscope; and yet he can nowhere find God. The patriarch anticipated him in this conclusion. He says that man, with all his boasted powers of insight, may search for Wisdom in the heaven above and the depth beneath, but whatever treasures he may find, this, which is the most precious treasure of all, will everywhere elude his grasp.* There is a mystery underlying all Nature, which, search as he may, remains undetected and incomprehensible. But to God, the Creator, all is known.† The profoundest mysteries of Nature are all open to Him, the methods of applying all its powers are wholly understood by Him. "God understandeth the way of wisdom, and He knoweth the place of understanding." And this wisdom which is His eternal perfection He has manifested in His creation. "He looketh to the ends of the earth; and seeth under the whole heaven: to make the weight for the winds; and He weigheth the waters by measure. When He made a decree for the rain, and a way for the lightning of the thunder; then did He see it, and declare it: He prepared it, yea, and searched it out." There is not a single adjustment, and "collocation" of the whole universe, which His infinite wisdom has not appointed and ordered. That wisdom includes the absolute knowledge of all natural causes and all natural effects, and governs them all. Even as regards natural things, man's knowledge is not only infinitesimally small compared with God's, but, yet

* Job xxviii. 12-14.   † Job xxviii. 23-28.

further, it is incapable of comprehending in any degree the mystery that lies behind Nature, the source and fountain head of the wisdom which Nature expresses. The only wisdom which can be of real spiritual value to man is of a different kind. "Unto man He said, Behold, the fear of the Lord, that is wisdom; and to depart from evil, that is understanding."

But this contrast between Divine wisdom and all that man can attain by his own investigations of nature, though so clearly expounded by the patriarch as evident, even in the most ordinary phenomena of nature, was nevertheless as yet little apprehended by him in its application to human life. He acknowledged in theory that there was this infinite difference between human wisdom and Divine; that to the latter all secret things were open, and that its range was unlimited, while the human mind was not only very limited in its range, but unable in the commonest things to penetrate to the hidden cause. And yet, while expounding this to others as undeniable truth, he proceeds to complain of the terrible afflictions that had come upon himself; who —as he appealed to all who knew him and to God Himself who knew all the secrets of his life—had served God in integrity of heart, and when he had offended, had not attempted to cover his transgressions, or hidden them in his own bosom. Nor was this a vainglorious boast, as it is with many who are righteous in their own eyes. The Lord Himself declared of Job, that there was none like him in the earth, "a perfect and an upright man, one that feareth God and escheweth evil."* But Job had not yet learnt the very truth which he himself expounded from creation, that the wisdom of God was beyond man's understanding. And therefore, although he had silenced his three friends,

* Job i. 8; li. 3.

who, in total ignorance of God's dealings with His children, had pointed to his sufferings, as proving that he was a hypocrite, and on that account punished; another* (Elihu) is raised up to speak to him in God's name, and teach him a further lesson. He reminds Job that if he fully acknowledges the infinite superiority of God to man, he ought to trust Him, though He gives no account of any of "His matters" to man. Often the severest chastisements are proofs of the tenderest love. To question God's justice because He sends us afflictions is to sin grievously against Him; it is in itself to "go in company with the workers of iniquity, and to walk with wicked men." God is the Judge of all the earth, and the Governor over all that He has created. His chastisements should lead us to humble ourselves before Him, even though our conscience accuses us of no sin. And to think otherwise of God is to be destitute of that which is the very beginning of all human wisdom, "the fear of God." And at last his argument brings the speaker back to the same theme from which Job himself had drawn the true conclusion as to the infinite wisdom of God. He points the patriarch to God's works in nature, and earnestly presses home the very lesson which he himself had expounded to his friends. Listen, he says, to the voice of God in nature, in which He thundereth marvellously with the voice of His excellency. "Great things doeth He, which we cannot comprehend." "Hearken unto this, O Job, stand still and consider the wondrous works of God. Dost thou know when God disposed them and caused the light of His cloud to shine? Dost thou know the balancings of the clouds, the wondrous works of Him which is perfect in knowledge?" And then having appealed, even as Job had done, to these universal proofs of God's wisdom

---

* Job xxxii. 6; xxxvii. 24.

in the order of His creation, as sufficient to make man feel that silence before Him is our truest wisdom, he draws the irresistible conclusion: "Touching the Almighty, we cannot find Him out: He is excellent in power and judgment, and plenty of justice; He will not afflict,"—without reason, or, as in the Septuagint, He will not give account to man. "Men therefore do fear Him; He respecteth not any that are wise of heart," in their own estimation. This conclusive moral and spiritual argument from God's works in Creation is followed by the voice of God Himself* speaking to Job out of the whirlwind: not arguing with His feeble and sinful creature as his fellow-men might argue, however wisely; but, with Divine authority, calling on him to answer to His Maker, and demanding of him his right to set up his ignorance against the wisdom of God. "Where wast thou when I laid the foundations of the earth? declare if thou hast understanding." One by one, from their beginning—"when the morning stars sang together, and all the sons of God shouted for joy," the marvellous works of God in Creation are enumerated. All these, from one end of the immeasurable universe to the other, from the greatest and most glorious of the creations in heaven to all the manifold forms of animal life on earth, are God's own work. They are beyond, not only the power of man to create, or even to control,—except as God gives him authority in a very limited sphere,—but also beyond his power to explain, so as to account for the absolute and ultimate reason of all the various and manifold phenomena of nature. The very commonest facts that meet man's eye in his daily life, the instincts, as we call them, of the beasts of the field and the birds of the air, as well as the beautiful variety and the wonderful vigour and energy of animal life, surpass the

* Job xxxviii., xxxix.

Creation the Work of Wisdom.

wisdom of man to account for. Well may man, whenever he does by faith realize in the simplest facts of nature the infinite wisdom of his Creator, feel as Job did before Him;* "Behold, I am vile : what shall I answer Thee? I will lay my hand upon my mouth. Once have I spoken, but I will not answer, yea, twice, but I will proceed no further."

Yet this lesson of simple, unreserved submission to God's will, as infinite alike in wisdom, justice, goodness, and power, needs to be thoroughly learnt by man if patience is to have its perfect work. And therefore the patriarch is finally reminded of the utter impotence of man in comparison with the strength even of those creatures of God, which though mere brute beasts, yet ought to be outward and visible witnesses to us of our insignificance, notwithstanding all our boasted skill, and our superiority as reasonable beings. Of such a creature of God (whatever may be the "leviathan" here described) He says, "None is so fierce that dare stir him up; who then is able to stand before Me?"† With this Divine Voice from Nature itself, revealing to him at once the infinite and unsearchable wisdom, the unlimited and inexhaustible knowledge, and the greatness and almighty power of God as manifested in His works, before which the wisdom, understanding, and strength of man utterly shrivel into nothing and disappear, the humbled and penitent servant of God now completely and finally submits to God's will. "I have heard of Thee by the hearing of the ear, but now mine eye seeth Thee. Wherefore I abhor myself, and repent in dust and ashes."

* Job x. 4, 5.
† See Note D in Appendix.

CHAPTER V.

REASON THE LIGHT OF DIVINE WISDOM.

THE argument from Creation in the Book of Job, connected as it is with profound questions as to the wisdom and righteousness of the Creator, and the government of the world, which that infinite and omnipotent wisdom made and constituted as the habitation for the sons of men, touches the great theme of God's Creation in many points of deep and universal interest; as a brief examination of that argument has been sufficient to indicate. The general purpose of this part of Revelation is evidently to exhibit, in various directions of human thought, the infinite and essential superiority of God's wisdom and knowledge to all that man either possesses or can acquire. At the same time, while God's Spirit "Who spake by the prophets" reminds us in this book, that there are everywhere in God's works mysteries of wisdom, which are not merely unsearchable, because they are infinite in extent, but also such as cannot be expressed in any form of human thought, and therefore inconceivable by the mind of man; there are not a few intimations here, as we have also seen, that the actual manifestations of the wisdom of the Creator in nature around us in some respects resemble, far as they surpass, those which our own mind can appreciate; and therefore they may teach us, not as a mere theory or notion, but by comparison of ourselves with a standard which we find in every direction to be immeasurably superior to our own, how entirely unreserved must be our confidence in God, and how fully He understands all that is in man. The moral and spiritual conclusions from the revelation of God's wisdom in His works are derived, not merely from the infinite superiority of His wisdom, but also, and we may say equally, from that wisdom being, in not a few of its manifestations and operations, such as is intelligible to the human mind. It is this characteristic of Divine wisdom, I mean its relation to human wisdom, which we must now proceed to investigate further from the teaching of Scripture, in order that we may draw such conclusions as are in accordance with the Christian Faith as to the action of Divine wisdom in the creation of the universe.

This relation is (as we have before observed) explicitly manifested in the New Testament, through the revelation of the Eternal Word of God, Who, being the Creator, came into this world, and took the nature of man and dwelt among us. But even as, before the coming of Christ, there were many prophetical intimations of various parts of His redeeming work, which are very valuable aids to enable us to appreciate their force and meaning; so in regard to the true import of this Divine fact of the Word of God, Who has redeemed us, being our Creator, the Spirit of God has given us in Holy Scripture, especially in that portion of the Book of Proverbs to which I have before referred, a description of the actings of the Divine wisdom in the work of Creation, in which some of the relations of human wisdom with the Divine are not obscurely indicated.

(1) The Wisdom which is the theme of the Book of the Proverbs of Solomon, the son of David king of Israel, might be regarded merely as a poetic and prosopopœic representa-

tion of the attribute of Divine wisdom, were it not that the revelation in the Gospel of the *"Logos"* of God as the Only-begotten Son, Who was made man and became our Redeemer, has given a new force and reality to the personification, now that Christ has been manifested to man. This Wisdom is set forth in the Book of Proverbs as the one source to the sons of men of all blessings, and of all true honour and prosperity, temporal and eternal. "She is more precious than rubies, and all the things thou canst desire are not to be compared with her. Length of days is in her right hand, and in her left hand riches and honour. Her ways are ways of pleasantness, and all her paths are peace. She is a tree of life to them that lay hold upon her, and happy is every one that retaineth her."* And it must be observed, that this which is here represented as being in man so great a blessing is *the same wisdom as that by which God Himself created all things.* "The Lord by wisdom hath founded the earth; by understanding hath He established the heavens. By His knowledge the depths are broken up; and the clouds drop down the dew." The operations of what we call natural agencies belong to the same Divine wisdom. Indeed, considering wisdom, whether in God or man, as that universal reason which both seeks the best ends and employs the best means to attain them,† we must obviously infer that it includes in itself not only all moral and spiritual virtue, but equally all intellectual excellence. And in the Divine mind these are inseparably united.

That the wisdom of which the inspired writer speaks in this book includes that which we call intellectual, is evident from many other passages. Thus, in the eighth chapter ‡ it is said, "I wisdom dwell with prudence"—or practical judgment—"and find out knowledge of witty inventions,"

---
* Prov. iii. 15-18. † See p. 49, *supra*. ‡ Prov. viii. 12-16.

or rather, wise devices and counsels. And therefore in a following verse it is added, "By me kings reign and princes decree justice. By me princes rule, and nobles, all the judges of the earth." It was, in fact, specially to enable him to govern and judge the nation over which he was appointed to reign as the heir of David's throne, that Solomon asked for the gift of wisdom;* "Give me now," he prayed, "wisdom and knowledge, that I may go out and come in before Thy people." "Give Thy servant an understanding heart to judge Thy people, that I may discern between good and bad."† There can be no doubt that the wisdom for which Solomon asked, and which God gave him, while it was some of that very Divine wisdom which created the world, was emphatically *human* wisdom. "And God gave Solomon wisdom and understanding exceeding much, and largeness of heart, even as the sand that is on the sea shore. And Solomon's wisdom excelled the wisdom of the east country and all the wisdom of Egypt. For he was wiser than all men, ... and his fame was in all nations round about. And he spake three thousand proverbs, and his songs were a thousand and five. And he spake of trees, from the cedar tree that is in Lebanon even unto the hyssop that springeth out of the wall; he spake also of beasts and of fowls, and of creeping things and of fishes." ‡

It is well to present before our mind this description of the wisdom given by God to man out of the fulness of His own wisdom, so that we may distinctly recognize the truth that the wisdom of the Creator, however infinitely superior, yet in all those things with which man's finite reason can deal, *includes all human wisdom*, and is in one sense similar. We must not suppose that our scientific knowledge, for example—when it is truly the result of reason—is anything

* 2 Chron. i. 10.   † 1 Kings iii. 8.   ‡ 1 Kings iv. 29-33.

else than the result in us of the exercise of the wisdom that comes from God. In this as in other respects man is the image and likeness of His Creator. And in his wisdom we see an image, however faint and imperfect, and too often distorted, of the Divine.

We must not doubt that the likeness does really exist. But let us suppose the intellect of man, being cultivated from age to age without intermission, to be capable of retaining all that it learns, and to accumulate knowledge by perpetual progress; while it is ever acquiring fresh powers of assimilating and applying it. Let science be thus extended beyond the wildest dreams of the imagination, so as to be able to trace clearly the sequences of natural causes and effects to limits as yet unconceived; and further, by the vastly enlarged sphere of its vision, to determine the solution of problems in nature which as yet, from the complexity and multitude of the hitherto unknown quantities involved in them, are to our minds quite indeterminate: still, all this science, though, as compared with man's present attainments, it would seem infinitely great, yet compared with God's wisdom, would be as defective and insignificant as the knowledge of nature which the most ignorant peasant possesses. In the brightness of the light of the Divine wisdom all finite light is as the blackness of darkness.

But that which is all-important for us to remember is not merely that this wisdom is *in* God (that no one will question), but that *by this wisdom* all the works of God in nature were made. And let us consider what this implies. First of all, it certainly means, that the end being the creation of the heaven and the earth, and all things therein, God accomplished this end through such means, and by the operation of such causes, as were fitted to make it in accordance with His will. The discoveries of science are nothing more than traces

Reason the Light of Divine Wisdom. 61

which the cultivated reason of man discerns here and there in nature, of methods which the infinite wisdom of God, the Universal Reason, employed for the fulfilment of these ends. Far from the discovery of such physical causes being in any way contrary to our faith in the Creator, it is only a commentary on the very teaching of Holy Scripture, from which our faith is derived, that the heaven and the earth were created, not by almighty power alone, but equally by infinite wisdom.

(2) This truth—I mean, that the very being of God indicates that His creation would be effected according to reason; in other words, through processes and methods consistent with reason—is one which the more distinct and complete revelation in the New Testament of the mystery of the Father and the Son very emphatically confirms. For we have not now merely to infer, from the language of the Proverbs respecting the wisdom of God, and the character of the wisdom which in some special cases God gave to the children of men, that there is an intimate relation between human reason and Divine wisdom; but we have expressly revealed to us the only-begotten Son,* "the Word;" "Who was in the beginning with God, and was God." And He was *the Light of man, through the Life in Him.* Not only the spiritual light by which man knows God and has eternal life, but also the intellectual light of reason, by which man lives as a rational being, is of Him. He is the Divine and Eternal Wisdom of which the reason of man is the image and reflection. "*He was the true Light, that lighteth every man,* coming into the world." And the evangelist not only teaches that "all things were made by Him," but—as if there were danger of our overlooking this fundamental element in the Christian faith on the subject of creation, which

* John i. 1-10.

the Old Testament had but imperfectly shadowed forth in symbolical language suited for the dispensation of types and figures—he again expressly affirms, that *"without Him was not anything made that hath been made."* God never exercises His creating power except through the Word. " Through Him God made the ages." * " In Him were all things created, in the heavens and upon the earth . . . . all things have been created through Him and unto Him; and He is before all things, and in Him all things consist."†

It follows, then, that to imagine any work of God in creation to be a mere isolated act of absolute power, and not a work effected by, and according to, that wisdom of which the human mind partakes in the divine gift of Reason, would be contrary to that characteristic doctrine of the Christian Faith as to Creation, by which it is distinguished from the faith of the Old Dispensation, which only included the truth implicitly, and did not explicitly reveal it.

* Heb. i. 2. † Colos. i. 16, 17.

CHAPTER VI.

TEACHING OF ST. AUGUSTINE.

WITHOUT pursuing further at present this branch of our argument, it may be well here to pause and consider for a while, how far the views as to the Christian Faith on the subject of Creation, which we have endeavoured to expound in the preceding chapters, are in accordance with the teaching of the Church of Christ. Many adversaries of that faith, some of them of considerable scientific pretensions, contend that these are nothing more than adjustments and accommodations which have been forced upon us reluctantly by the discoveries of modern science, and not such as would, independently of such discoveries, have ever been allowed as legitimate interpretations of those Holy Scriptures from which our faith is derived.

Now it may be freely admitted that, so far as the popular theology of the period since the Reformation is concerned, there is considerable truth in this charge made by scientific infidelity. The natural tendency both of the Calvinistic theology generally, and specially of its excessive reverence for the letter of Holy Scripture, was no doubt to cramp the exercise of the higher reason in its interpretation of Scripture, and to treat articles of faith, and doctrines generally, as dogmas rather than living truths. And of this Puritanical theology, the great Milton was the poet. His " Paradise

Lost" gives an interpretation of the inspired history of creation in accordance with the strictest literal notions. What is more fatal to its truth as a Christian exposition of this Divine work, is that it presents a picture of the exercise of power quite independently of all rational means, that is, independently of wisdom. The genius of Calvinism is in fact familiar with this view of God as mere Sovereignty. Creation in Milton's poem is nothing else than an unconnected series of marvellous acts of power. And there can be no doubt that the majestic poetry of the Puritan bard has done more than anything else to stereotype, in the Christian thought of Protestantism, the hard-and-fast literal, or rather unspiritual and unchristian, notions as to creation, to which so many cling as if they were the only true revelation of God. Professor Huxley has been blamed, quite unreasonably, for having in his American addresses on Evolution spoken of the literal interpretation of the first chapter of Genesis as the " Miltonic hypothesis," and kept it quite distinct from the Biblical account. But Professor Huxley, in making this distinction, merely follows writers on the Christian side, who, long before those addresses were delivered by him, had pointed out how much of the popular belief about Creation was due to the untheological poetry of Milton. And there is no doubt whatever that we owe a deep debt of gratitude to modern science,—to astronomy, to geology, and last, though not least of all, to evolution, so far as it is really scientific,—for setting Christian thought in the present day free from the bondage to the letter to which Calvinism had partially enslaved it. The objections against the Christian faith on the subject of Creation, which the discoveries of science have suggested, have no doubt been beneficial to Christianity, in the same manner as the various heresies that have assailed the faith from age to age have ultimately confirmed and elucidated it. They have compelled Christians to study Holy Scripture more carefully and more widely, and the result is that the faith has been held at last more intelligently, and therefore more distinctly, than ever.

But if the scientific opponents of the Christian faith as to Creation suppose, that the broader and larger and truer views of God's works, those which are indeed alone worthy of the greatness, and glory, and (most of all) of the wisdom of the infinite Creator, have been due to themselves and not to God's Word, there is abundantly sufficient testimony to the contrary to refute them. For these views, in their substance, were held and taught by Christian theologians, long before any of these sciences, as they are received in modern times, had a beginning. Of all the early Christian writers, none has discussed the Christian faith on the subject of Creation so fully, so profoundly, and in such a truly philosophical spirit,—as, almost universally during one period, to guide Christian thought,—as St. Augustine of Hippo. This great man was not only the most illustrious of all the Latin fathers, but the first Christian writer after the apostolic age who was a profound thinker; one who could sympathize with the intellectual difficulties of others as to the teaching of the Church, and was therefore best qualified to deal with them.

He was prepared for the special work to which God called him, not only by a liberal education in rhetoric and philosophy in his youth, but yet more through having in early manhood embraced the heresy of Manichæism; the doctrines of which seem, like other visionary systems of error in later ages, to have had a strange fascination for those ardent and imaginative minds, in whom the religious sentiment is stronger than the sense of personal responsibility to God. When, after some years' experience of this heresy, he began to distrust its teaching, he still, though now attracted towards the Christian faith, was prevented from accepting it by metaphysical difficulties, chiefly as to the mystery of the origin of evil. In the struggles of his soul at that time, which he touchingly describes in his "Confessions," nothing, he says, would have saved him from falling into utter Atheism except the deep inward conviction of judgment after death, which he could not shake off. It is very instructive to observe how in such a mind intellectual and moral difficulties were always associated together; and that the one solution for both was faith in Christ as the "Word of God." He acknowledges the goodness of God in providentially putting in his way at this time a Latin translation of some of the Platonic writers, which prepared his mind for the reception of Christian truth, especially on the subject of the Incarnation of the Word of God. This fundamental truth of Christianity, which he found in the teaching of St. John, was to him indeed a light from heaven; a revelation which testified for itself to his own conscience, and required no external evidence. And little by little that light shone brighter and clearer in his heart, and before it all the intellectual and moral difficulties gradually vanished away. In his thirty-fourth year he was received by baptism into the Church of Christ. One of his early works, written a few years after his baptism, but before his ordination to the priesthood, was a "Treatise on the Book of Genesis," specially directed against the errors of the Manichæans, who denied that the God of the Old Testament was the same as the God and Father Whom Christ revealed. It seems that the account of Creation given in the first two chapters of Genesis was with them as favourite a subject for ridicule and cavils, as it is among infidels in the present

Teaching of St. Augustine.

day, though not on the same grounds. He remarks that their attacks on Holy Scripture do, indeed, too often shake the faith of the feeble and unstable, and yet are overruled for good, both by awakening us to the necessity of a fuller knowledge of Scripture, and enabling us to teach others more fully the way of truth.

In this treatise, composed before he had fully examined and considered the teaching of the Scriptures on Creation, he acknowledges that he found almost insuperable difficulties in the literal, as contrasted with the allegorical interpretations of Holy Scripture.* He observes that those who examine this part of Revelation with pious diligence propose even more questions to solve than the adversaries of the faith themselves can suggest; but the former seek that they may find, whereas the only object of the others is to find difficulties which cannot be solved, and thus to bring discredit on Holy Scripture. He observes that if any one wishes to take its teaching literally, and can so interpret it consistently with reverence to God and with the Catholic Faith, such an one is not only to be envied, but ought to be considered as the best and most praiseworthy interpreter. But Augustine evidently at that time saw no such solution himself, and doubted whether such was possible. And if there is no other course left, so as to understand what is written piously and worthily of God, except by supposing the history to be set forth as a figure and allegory, we are (he says) fully authorized by the example of the apostles, who adduced so many things from the Old Testament as types and figures of better things to come, to use the history for this purpose, at all events for the present, without prejudicing any better and more careful investigation of the

* "De Genesi contra Manichæos," lib. ii., § ii. Note E in Appendix.

subject, either by ourselves or any others to whom God may reveal it.*

Although, however, the reply that might be sufficient for the objections of the Manichæans would hardly be suitable for those of modern infidelity, there is one illustration that Augustine uses in this treatise which he further expands in subsequent writings on the same subject, and which contains a principle of interpretation that almost startles us by its conformity with modern scientific thought. He is explaining how the words, "*In the beginning God created the heavens and the earth*," may be applicable to the whole of the subsequent creation. This, he says, is true, not because the creation existed already, but because it *could be*, it *existed potentially*. "For as if we consider the seed of a tree, we may say that there are in it the roots, and the branch, and the fruit, and the leaves; not because they exist already, but because they are to come into existence from that seed;" so it is said, "'*In the beginning God made the heaven and the earth*'; as if this were the *seed* of the heaven and the earth, although as yet all the material of heaven and earth was in confusion; but because it was certain that from this the heaven and the earth would be, therefore the material itself is called by that name."†

Four or five years after this work was published, and while he was still a presbyter of the Church, Augustine began a work on Genesis, such as he felt was required, in which the history might be investigated without having recourse to allegorical interpretation. But he found himself at that time of his life still unequal to the task; "In Scripturis exponendis tirocinium meam sub tantæ sarcinæ mole succubuit, et non dum perfecto uno libro, ab eo quem

* Note F in Appendix.
† "De Genes. contra Man.," lib. l., § vii.   Note G in Appendix.

sustinere non poteram labore conquievi,"* he says in his "Retractations," and the work was left unfinished. He afterwards wrote twelve books on the same subject, and although, even in these, he acknowledges, many questions are rather proposed as subjects for investigation than as capable of being thoroughly explained; yet he considers them far superior to his unfinished work, which he leaves, he says, chiefly as an indication, which might not be without use, of his rudimentary thoughts in the investigation of the Divine oracles. These works together must be taken as containing his matured views as to the true teaching of the inspired history of creation, without treating it as an allegory. And while he now does not find it necessary to take refuge in allegorical meanings in order to interpret the history consistently with the infinite perfections of God, yet he recognizes, what in his first treatise on this subject he does not seem to have realized, that its language must, from the necessity of the case, be not literal, in the usual sense of the word, but *symbolical or ideal* language, such as is adapted to convey to our limited and imperfect apprehensions those conceptions of the Divine working which may most impress our hearts with the mysteries of His Divine wisdom and power, and of His eternal and infinite Being; and at the same time indicate the intimate connection between the mystery of Creation and that of Redemption.

He gives some practical cautions as to the study of such parts of Holy Scripture as treat of obscure subjects wholly removed from the range of our understandings, which cautions it would be well if theologians of all ages had more carefully observed. The first is† that when passages

* "Retract.," lib. i., cap. xviii.
† "De Gen. ad Litteram," i., § 37.

of Holy Scripture can, without imperilling the faith, yield different meanings, we must not so commit ourselves hastily and dogmatically to any one particular view that our whole argument breaks down if further and more careful investigation of truth shall overthrow our particular interpretation. We are too ready to act, he says, as if we were contending, not for the meaning which Holy Scripture itself contains, but for our own, and as though our wish were that the sense of Scripture should be that which we adopt; whereas our desire ought rather to be to adopt as our own that which is the meaning of Scripture. He gives, as an instance, the various meanings that might be given to the light which is described as being created by the Word of God. But he also points to another more general case* in which serious injury may, and often does, arise to the cause of Christianity from partial dealing with the Word of God. "It very often happens," he says, "that there is some question as to the earth, or the sky, or the other elements of this world, as to the motion or course, or even the magnitude and distance, of the heavenly bodies, the cycles of years and seasons, of the nature of animals, trees, stones, or other things of this kind, respecting which one who is not a Christian has knowledge derived from most certain reasoning or observation." In fact, a scientific man. "And it is very disgraceful and mischievous, and of all things to be carefully avoided, that a Christian speaking about such matters as if according to the Christian Scriptures, should be heard by an unbeliever talking such nonsense that the unbeliever, perceiving him to be as wide from the mark as east from west, can hardly restrain himself from laughing. And it is not merely that an ignorant man is ridiculed, but that our authors are believed by those who

* Lib. i., § 39. Note H in Appendix.

are without to have held such opinions, and are found fault with and rejected as unlearned men, to the loss of the souls of those for whose salvation we are earnestly striving." He proceeds to say that these rash and self-appointed champions of the truth, who set up their own hasty conclusions from Holy Scripture as the very Word of God itself, little know what trouble and sorrow they cause their more prudent brethren. Alas! the scene described here repeats itself in the nineteenth century, with some differences as to the questions in regard to which the unbeliever ridicules the ignorance of the Christian, but in substance precisely the same.

It is evident that the principles here laid down by Augustine could not fail to be adverse to narrow and irrational interpretations of this part of Holy Scripture, and to lead the student to regard the spirit, and not the mere letter, as expressing the truth. In referring to the apparent contradictions in Gen. ii. 4, which speaks of "'*the day*' *in which God made the heaven and the earth*," whereas in the first chapter the Sacred Record had spoken of six days altogether, he points out the impossibility of there being measurements of time before those motions of created things existed which determine and measure time, and he continues :* "Wherefore when we consider the original condition of the things created, from which works of His God rested on the seventh day, we ought not to think either of those days as being these solar days of ours, nor of the working of God itself as now God works anything in time; but rather as He has worked from Whom time itself had its beginning, as He has worked all things simultaneously"— in the sense which he explains in his former treatise (see p. 68); "bringing them also into due order, not by intervals

* "De Genes. ad Lit.," lib. v. cap. v. Note I in Appendix.

of time, but by connexion of causes, so that those things which in the mind of God were made simultaneously, might be brought to their completion by the six-fold representation of that one day. It was therefore not by the order of a succession of times, but by the order of a succession of causes, that there was first made the substance without form, and capable of being brought into form, whether spiritual or material, from which should be created that which was to be created." And again, after enumerating the works of the six days as described in the first chapter of Genesis, he continues: "All this order of the creation wrought into its order that one day knew; and by this knowledge being six times in some way or other exhibited, showed forth as it were six days—although it was in another sense only one day—by recognizing those things which were made, primarily in the creation and then in the things themselves by consequence, and yet not remaining in the things themselves, but referring also the subsequent knowledge of them to the love of God, and so made an evening, morning, and midday in all; not by prolongation of time, but by means of the order of things created."*

The exact meaning of this passage of St. Augustine, the metaphysical argument in which we shall refer to in a following chapter,† it is unnecessary to discuss; it is sufficient to observe that both the language itself of the sacred record, and yet more his own profound sense of the impossibility of representing in the forms of finite thought the operations of the infinite and eternal Mind, compelled this great theologian to look beyond the mere letter of the inspired history of creation; and at a time when the objections which science has since suggested against the

* Lib. v., § 15.
† See Part II., chap. ii.

Teaching of St. Augustine. 73

literal interpretation of Gen. i. could not possibly have been anticipated, to indicate principles of interpretation which supply by anticipation, not only a reply to all such objections, but also very valuable guidance when we compare other conclusions of modern science with this teaching of Holy Scripture.

For these principles extend far beyond the mere question of the length of the period of Creation, as even the passages already quoted sufficiently show. As he says, it is not a question of time, but of the *order of causation* in the mind and wisdom of God, and, as he argues,—and this indeed lies at the root of the whole question of the interpretation of the history of Creation,—the truth is, " That he who creates the causes creates *at the same time* in them all the effects of these causes." This is implied, Augustine points out, in the remarkable words of the Sacred Record which (Gen. ii. 4, 5) speak of the day that the Lord God made the earth and the heavens, and every plant of the field *before it was in the earth*, and every herb of the field *before it grew*." He made the causes, and both imparted to them, and sustained in them, their efficacy, which He alone can do; and in doing this He is the Creator of all, and as He is the Creator so also the Governor.

The work of Creation he again * copiously illustrates from the growth of a tree from its seed, in which are originally all its various branches and other parts, which do not suddenly spring up such and so large as they are when complete, but in that order with which we are familiar in nature. All these things are in the seed, not by material substance, *but by causal energy and potency*. "And," he proceeds afterwards to say, " even so as in the grain itself there were invisibly all things simultaneously, which were

* Lib. v., cap. xxiii.

in time to grow into the tree, so the world itself is to be thought of, when God simultaneously created all things, as having at the same time in itself all things that were made in it and with it, when the day itself was created: not only the heaven, with the sun and moon and stars, etc., but also those things which the water and the earth produced *potentialiter atque causaliter*, before that, in due time, and after long delays, they grew up in such manner as they are now known to us in those works of God which He is working even to the present hour."

This principle of the creation of the causes and potencies being the creation of all the subsequent development from them, however long the time may be that is required for that development, is in fact that which Augustine applies to the whole account of Creation, and by which he attempts to solve all the difficulties in the history. And it must be remembered, that this is not only the profound conclusion of a philosophical mind, but is involved of necessity in the very idea of Creation as revealed in Holy Scripture and the object of faith. The truth is not merely that God *was*, but that He *is* the Creator. The natural causes, in the order He appointed, not only derived originally all their potency from Him, but retain that potency solely through His Divine power. So Jesus Christ, the Word of God in our nature, said in reference to the Sabbath day, "My Father worketh hitherto, and I work"—although the original work of Creation ceased on the seventh day—"and I work," that is, by the Divine Energy still maintaining the operations of Nature. "For in Him," St. Paul says,[*] "*all things consist*."

So far then as regards the argument, that modern science has compelled Christians to do violence to Holy Scripture,

[*] Col. i. 17.

Teaching of St. Augustine. 75

the fact that such interpretations as these of St. Augustine were given and accepted, without the slightest reference either to the theories of modern science or to any other (*e.g.*, of ancient Greek philosophy), but simply as conclusions to which the Christian mind was directed by the language of that part of Scripture, read in the light of the complete Revelation of God in His Word, is sufficient reply. But it must be observed that the principle which he accepts, as involved in the very history of Creation, is of such primary importance in regard to the Christian Faith on the subject of Creation, that it will require separate consideration.*

* Note J in Appendix.

CHAPTER VII.

TRUE IDEA OF CREATION.

THE complete idea of Creation, as indeed Holy Scripture teaches throughout, includes not merely the first constitution of the world and the whole Universe, but all that to the present day is in Creation and of Creation, as the result of all the various causes and energies and potencies which God has called into operation and continues to maintain in Nature. God's Creation is not a *machine* made by almighty power and wisdom, and thenceforward working automatically to produce results other than the Creation itself. Nor is the Creator revealed as the First Cause, merely connected with His Universe by a chain of innumerable sequences of causes and effects, but as the living God, equally present at all times and through all the most varied results of these sequences, which are, without exception, His works. The whole of Nature is His creation not only as it was at first, but as much now in its present form and aspect. In all its uses and appliances and adaptations, God is all and in all. Every man who is born into the world is as truly God's creation as Adam and Eve were at the first. When the Psalmist says of himself, "I will praise Thee, for I am fearfully and wonderfully made. Thine eyes did see my substance yet being imperfect: and in Thy book all my members were written which in continuance were fashioned

True Idea of Creation. 77

when as yet there was none of them;"* does he not realize that he was as completely the work of the Creator's power and wisdom as if he had been the first man that God created? The fact that the will of man, by rebelling against his Maker's law, had introduced disorder into the work of God, did not make that which was God's creation any the less certainly His. Nor does the fact that the labour of man, whom God created and placed on the earth to replenish it and subdue it, has in many respects changed the face of Nature and modified many of the productions of Nature, and directed to his own purposes many of its energies, affect in the least degree the truth that all are the creatures of God.

No more striking illustration of this can be found in Holy Scripture than in that glorious Nature Psalm, the hundred and fourth, which has been called † "the first chapter of Genesis set to music." It is indeed impossible to doubt that the description of the Creation contained in that chapter is present to the mind of the Psalmist. The whole of the six days' work is included in this Divine poem, though not in exactly the same order as in Genesis; because the inspired author has specially in view Creation *as it is*, fulfilling the purposes for which it is made, rather than as it was constituted at the first. He begins by praising the Lord, Whose glorious creation of the visible universe is the vesture in which He, Whom human eyes cannot behold, has clothed Himself. The created light which His Word in the beginning called forth out of darkness and chaos is to us the sign and representation of that spiritual Light which no man can approach unto, but it is in itself but the garment which veils from our vision His own Divine glory. His works in the heaven above and the earth beneath are per-

* Psalm cxxxix. 14-16.
† Bishop Wordsworth.

petual* manifestations of the Divine Majesty of Him Who is Himself invisible. He stretcheth out the canopy of the firmament as His own pavilion; the beams of His chambers are laid in the waters; the clouds are His royal chariot; the winds of heaven are the wings which bear Him from land to land, or He makes them His messengers to convey His commands; and the lightnings His ministers to execute His will. But God Himself, Whose creations these are, is hidden from our view, though He is ever present, and ever manifesting His own power and divinity in His works. He at the first divided the sea and the dry land, and made the great mountains to rise out of the deep, the waters of which at His command hasted to find in the valleys the bounds appointed for them, while the rivers ran among the hills. And thus this earth was prepared to produce the sustenance which God by such means continually provides for the beasts of the field and the fowls of the air, as well as for man, the lord of creation. He continually watereth the hills from His chambers. "He causeth the grass to grow for the cattle, and herb for the service of man; that He may bring forth food out of the earth, and wine that maketh glad the heart of man, and oil to make his face to shine, and bread which strengtheneth man's heart." Then, after other examples of the wisdom of God, in the adaptations of the world which He created to the uses for which it was intended and ordered, we are reminded that the periodical return of day and night has its purpose in the order of man's own life. "Man goeth forth to his work and to his labour until the evening." And filled with admiration of the goodness and wisdom of the Creator, the Psalmist says, "O

---

* "In the Hebrew, the words rendered *coverest Thyself*, *stretchest out*, etc., express the original act of creation, and also the perpetual maintaining power of God." (Commentary by the late Dean of Wells.)

Lord, how manifold are Thy works! in wisdom hast Thou made them all; the earth is full of Thy riches. So is this great and wide sea, wherein are things creeping innumerable, both small and great beasts. There go the ships, there is that leviathan, whom Thou hast made to play therein."

It will be observed that here, while the original acts of creation are undoubtedly the primary theme of the psalm, the whole of Nature, and of its life and uses, is included. The riches of which the earth is full are God's; they are *His* works, *His* gifts, *His* ordinances; just as truly His creation as if they had been made originally, by a supernatural act of Divine power, in the forms and with the uses with which we are now familiar; instead of having become what they are through the effects of natural causes that have been in operation for ages past.

Our faith, then, in God as the Creator is not a belief either in a "Great Architect," as though He were one who built up the universe by a series of supernatural acts of Divine power lasting through a limited period; or in a "First Cause," as if He stood first in a succession of causes, from which He differed only in being the most comprehensive of all, the Cause of all other causes, a kind of universal "force behind nature," as some have said; but in the Living God, Who is both infinite and eternal, the same from everlasting to everlasting. On the other hand, while the faith which is derived from Revelation is clearly and sharply distinguished from the creed of Pantheism, whether that creed be that the universe is God, or that God is the universe; yet we know that God is present throughout His universe, with the selfsame power, wisdom, and energy, by which that universe was made at the beginning; so that the whole earth is His, and the fulness thereof.

While, however, the idea of Creation which Holy Scripture presents to us, and which faith apprehends, is thus comprehensive, it must be remembered that there are certain distinctions necessary to be observed, in order that our faith on the subject of Creation may be more definite. We believe in God as Creator, primarily, as the Eternal and Infinite Mind, in Which—before time was, or any of those things that exist actually under conditions of time and space—all that was to be hereafter manifested was formed. It is in reference to this, which we may call the primary sense of Creation, that the Sacred Record speaks of the created existences being made before there began to be any natural development of them whatever.*

Then there was Creation in its secondary sense, when that which existed in the Eternal Mind began to be manifested in the "æons," or under the condition of time; and when the order of the universe was developed through the operation of those physical causes and energies, originating in the Divine power and wisdom, in which the whole has its subsistence.

But again, in this Creation, in its secondary sense, there is a distinction drawn in the teaching of Scripture. There is a period, called in the Book of Genesis *the six days*, in which "the heavens and the earth were finished, and all the host of them;" or, "*the day* in which the Lord God made the earth and the heaven;" and in the New Testament "the creation,"† or "the foundation of the world;"‡ or, in the Epistle to the Hebrews, as we have seen § already, "the æons," during which there was the

---

* Gen. ii. 4, 5.
† Mark x. 6, xiii. 19; Rom. i. 20; 2 Peter iii. 4.
‡ καταβολὴ κόσμου. Matt. xiii. 35; Luke xi. 50; Heb. iv. 3, ix. 26, etc.
§ See Chap. I., p. 16, *supra*.

genesis of "the heaven and earth," until it had its consummation in the creation of man. And although, as we have found, all the subsequent results of the Creator's power and wisdom, through the operation of those physical forces by which He still acts in nature, are no less truly His creation, having equally originated in the Divine Logos; yet there is obviously a distinction drawn, as regards the manifestation of creating power. In fact, the one is the Day of the Working of God in Creation, the other of God's Rest.

I do not here enter into any question as to the identity, or the difference, of the physical causes in operation during the period of Genesis, and subsequently to it; for this is a question which we may consider with more advantage in the second part of this treatise.* For the present, I simply point out the distinctions that Holy Scripture itself indicates.

* See Part II., chap. viii.

CHAPTER VIII.

CREATION SUBJECTED TO VANITY.

THERE is one part of the Christian faith on the subject of Creation to which I think sufficient attention has never been given by theologians. And instructive as it is in itself, as connected with our faith on redemption, it has become in modern times specially important in its relation to the progress of science; and it is one in which, perhaps more than in any other direction whatever, science has proved itself the serviceable handmaid of faith, instead of being its rival and adversary. I refer to the view of Creation which St. Paul sets forth in the eighth chapter of his Epistle to the Romans, in which chapter he brings to its climax and glorious consummation the argument which he had commenced in the fifth chapter of that epistle, as to the victory through Christ of righteousness over sin, grace over wrath and condemnation, and life over death. It will be observed that, after reminding us* that the condition on which we are made joint-heirs with Christ is, "*If so be that we suffer with Him, that we may be also glorified with Him;*" he adds, as though to teach us how reasonable such a condition is, "*For I reckon that the sufferings of this present time are not worthy to be compared with the glory which shall be revealed*

* Rom. viii. 17-18.

Creation subjected to Vanity.

to us-ward." And in order to illustrate further both the harmony of such a condition with God's work as Creator, and the greatness and glory of the hope, as that in which the whole visible creation has an interest, he continues (I take the translation in the Revised Version), "*For the earnest expectation of the creation waiteth for the revealing of the sons of God. For the creation was subjected to vanity, not of its own will, but by reason of Him who subjected it, in hope that the creation itself also shall be delivered from the bondage of corruption into the liberty of the glory of the children of God. For we know that the whole creation groaneth and travaileth in pain together until now.*"* This passage is of so much importance that for convenience of reference the original Greek is given at length below. Now that the word (κτίσις) is here used in its ordinary sense, and includes all the material creation, animate and inanimate, is evident from the context. It answers as nearly as possible to "*Nature*" in our modern use of the word. There are numerous instances in Scripture itself of the personification of Nature, as sympathizing with man, and partaking both of his sorrows and his hopes. Thus Isaiah, describing the blessedness of God's redeemed,† says, "The mountains and the hills shall break forth before you into singing, and all the trees of the field shall clap their hands. Instead of the thorn shall come up the fir tree, and instead of the brier shall come up the myrtle tree." Which evidently means, not some change in the material productions of the earth, but the subjective change

---

* Rom. viii. 19-22:—Ἡ γὰρ ἀποκαραδοκία τῆς κτίσεως τὴν ἀποκάλυψιν τῶν υἱῶν τοῦ Θεοῦ ἀπεκδέχεται. τῇ γὰρ ματαιότητι ἡ κτίσις ὑπετάγη οὐχ ἑκοῦσα, ἀλλὰ διὰ τὸν ὑποτάξαντα, ἐπ' ἐλπίδι, ὅτι καὶ αὐτὴ ἡ κτίσις ἐλευθερωθήσεται ἀπὸ τῆς δουλείας τῆς φθορᾶς εἰς τὴν ἐλευθερίαν τῆς δόξης τῶν τέκνων τοῦ Θεοῦ. οἴδαμεν γὰρ ὅτι πᾶσα ἡ κτίσις συστενάζει καὶ συνωδίνει ἄχρι τοῦ νῦν.

† Isa. lv. 12-13.

in those who "go out with joy and are led forth with peace." The most distinct illustration, however, in Holy Scripture, of St. Paul's language, is that which is supplied by the description given in the Apocalypse,* of all creation praising God for the blessings of redemption. There St. John says, "Every created thing which is in the heaven and on the earth, and under the earth and on the sea, and all that are in them, heard I saying, Unto Him that sitteth on the throne, and unto the Lamb, be the blessing, and the honour, and the glory, and the dominion, for ever and ever." And here, as in St. Paul's description of the hopes of creation, πᾶν κτίσμα (which answers to πᾶσα ἡ κτίσις) does not include either the redeemed from all nations who are made "kings and priests unto God," or the angels in heaven, both of which classes are mentioned separately.† The passage in the Apocalypse is, indeed, an exact counterpart to that in the Epistle to the Romans, and must guide us in its interpretation. But although creation is in both these passages personified, yet St. Paul reminds us that it was not "through its own will" that it was subjected to vanity; which means, I conceive, not merely that all creation abhors, so to speak, the natural evils of decay and death to which it is subject, and every living creature resists it, and flies from it; but its condition was not due, as those evils are due from which man suffers, to a will that chose, as man's will chose, vanity rather than good, and death instead of life.

But, to see fully what is the force of the argument, it is necessary to consider what is the meaning of the words that "the creation was subjected to vanity." There can be no doubt that in using these the apostle had in his mind, which was full of Old Testament thought and feeling, that which is

* Rev. v. 3. † Rev. v. 9-12.

the key-note of the Book of Ecclesiastes, "Vanity of vanities, saith the preacher, vanity of vanities, all is vanity."* And this the preacher finds true, first of all, in the instability of all created things. Nature is ever repeating herself: she makes no progress, though she is always changing; the course of nature is a constant succession of events recurring in the same cycle; it is, as both *natura* in Latin and φύσις in Greek imply, a continual birth of phenomena succeeding continual dissolution. And this the apostle calls bondage to the law of *decay*. For "decay" expresses the idea more truly than "corruption," connected as that word is in English with repulsive associations not necessarily included in the meaning of the Greek word φθορά, which is nothing more than the opposite to γένεσις. The creation is subject to the necessity of continual "decaying" followed by continual "becoming." Γένεσις followed by φθορά, and φθορά by a new γένεσις, is the endless law; no rest, nothing satisfying.

But it may be asked why is this law, which certainly indicates an imperfect condition, imposed upon the work of an infinitely wise and almighty Creator? The apostle does not expressly answer this question; he merely says that it was not on account of any will in nature itself opposed to the Will of the Creator, that He brought it into subjection; but it was simply "*by reason of Him that subjected it;*" that is, of the Creator Himself: and he further adds that it was made subject to vanity, "in the hope that the creation itself also shall be" in God's appointed time "delivered from the bondage to this law of decay into the liberty of the glory of the sons of God."

The purpose with which the apostle introduces this allusion to the visible universe of God in his argument as to

* Eccles. i. 2, 14, iii. 19, xii. 8.

the final redemption of the sons of God from their present state, in which they are themselves in bondage to sin and death, is thus far sufficiently obvious. Creation itself is subjected to vanity as yet, but there is a prospect of a glorious regeneration of all creation—when there shall be new heavens and a new earth wherein dwelleth righteousness, suited for God's redeemed, whose future glorified state shall be free not from death only, but from all the evils to which nature in its original form has been liable.* But in order that this aspect of the Christian faith on the subject of creation may become more distinct, it is necessary to inquire further into the meaning of this remarkable and interesting passage of Holy Scripture. Does the apostle here, in thus describing the present condition of nature, (1) merely refer, as Solomon does apparently in the Book of Ecclesiastes, to that which is every man's own experience in this world in regard to natural things? or (2) is he referring to that which had been previously revealed respecting the creation of God? or (3) is he here himself, by the Holy Spirit, revealing some new truths, supplementary to that which had been already known? Instead of giving a categorical reply to these questions, it will be better to take a comprehensive view of the subject in all its relations.

It is, I think, impossible not to suppose that St. Paul, in this passage, had present to his mind that history of the Fall of Man, which in Holy Scripture immediately follows the history of Creation, and stands in the closest possible connexion with it, so that one is hardly intelligible apart from the other. And not only is the history of the Old Testament interwoven throughout with the whole of St. Paul's argument in this Epistle to the Romans, but, as was observed before,

* Rev. vii. 16; *cf.* Isa. xlix. 10.

Creation subjected to Vanity. 87

the particular argument, which is completed in this eighth chapter, commences in the fifth with a reference to the Fall and its consequences. In that chapter* there is the very same contrast, of a subjection to the bondage of corruption, and a deliverance unto a glorious life; only *there* the argument is confined to man, who came under that bondage through his own wilful transgression of a law of God; *here* it is extended to creation, which was subjected thereto through no will of its own. There we are reminded that through one man sin entered into the world, and death through sin; and so death passed unto all men, for that all sinned; since sin was in the world from the time of the Fall, even before the law was given through Moses, although sin is not counted as a wilful transgression, and punished as such, where there is no law. But that sin was actually present from the day when Adam fell is evident, he reminds us, from the fact that death reigned from that time over all his descendants, even over those that had not sinned, as he sinned, by a conscious and wilful transgression of a command of God. For the nature of man, having in their first father and by his sin lost the supernatural gift of life, became thenceforward subject, as all the rest of creation was from its first origin, to vanity and the bondage of corruption. But "where sin abounded, grace abounded yet more exceedingly; that as sin reigned in death, even so might grace reign through righteousness unto eternal life through Jesus Christ our Lord."

It would be impossible, I say, without confusing the whole argument, not to recognize the parallel of the contrast in the eighth chapter with this, which had been previously drawn in the fifth. And in the Divine judgments pronounced after the Fall,† we find the elements of the

* Rom. v. 12, etc.   † Gen. iii. 14-19.

whole subject to which St. Paul refers in both passages. In the judgment passed on the serpent,—the earthly representative of the Tempter,—a conflict is foretold between the adversary of man and the seed of the woman, in which a complete and final victory should be gained over the Evil One after a time of suffering: "He shall bruise thy head, and thou shalt bruise His heel." In the judgment on the woman, whose seed should overcome at the last, there is a sentence of mingled blessing and suffering: "I will greatly multiply thy sorrow and thy conception; in sorrow shalt thou bring forth children." And woman suffering in childbirth, till her hour of deliverance has come, is taken by St. Paul to represent "the whole creation groaning and travailing in pain till the day when the sons of God shall be revealed." While the judgment on man expressly includes inanimate nature: "Cursed is the ground for thy sake; in sorrow shalt thou eat of it all the days of thy life; thorns also and thistles shall it bring forth to thee; and thou shalt eat the herb of the field; in the sweat of thy brow shalt thou eat bread, till thou return unto the ground; for out of it wast thou taken; for dust thou art, and unto dust thou shalt return."

But it must be observed that while we have presented to us here the same general idea of a state of conflict with evil and suffering, and even apparent and temporary defeat, terminating in a glorious triumph of life over death, there is nothing to indicate that the subjection of the creation to the law of decay and death was the result of man's transgression, as it was to man himself. Man had been the one exception to the universal law of nature; and his exemption from that law, given him supernaturally, he forfeited by his sin, the act of his own will, and he could not regain that freedom except through redemption. How, then, are we to understand, as both the teaching of St. Paul and also the language of the Book of Genesis equally imply, that there is nevertheless an intimate connection between the condition of all creation as subject to a law of decay from the first, even prior to the entering of sin into the world, and the transgression of Adam? The answer to this is supplied by other teaching of Holy Scripture, especially of the New Testament; and this answer is not only sufficient and complete, but it enables us to perceive the full force and consistency of the apostle's argument. On the other hand, it expounds fully this particular aspect of the Christian Faith on the subject of creation, which it is most necessary to take into consideration, in reference to various objections against that faith which have been raised by infidelity.

In a passage in the Book of Proverbs,* to which we have referred already for another purpose, we are reminded that *Wisdom* was "*with God,*" as St. John also says of the "Logos," "*in the beginning before His works of old.*" "*I was set up,*" Wisdom says (or, as some translate the Hebrew, *I was anointed*), "*from everlasting, from the beginning, or ever the earth was.*" The Wisdom by which God made the heaven and the earth was Eternal Wisdom, to which all that should come to pass in the ages to come was perfectly known from the beginning to the end, or, as it is expressed in the ninetieth Psalm, "*Before the mountains were brought forth, or ever Thou hadst formed the earth and the world, from everlasting to everlasting Thou art God.*"† That Wisdom, then, which created all things with this perfect foreknowledge, created them as the scene in which there would be this conflict between Evil and Good, and in which there would be the final and glorious victory gained by the Divine Redeemer,

---

* Prov. viii. 22, etc.

* καὶ ἀπὸ τοῦ αἰῶνος, καὶ ἕως τοῦ αἰῶνος σὺ εἶ, ὁ θεός. LXX.

who in the fulness of time would take on Himself the nature of man, "*in order that through death He might bring to nought him that had the power of death, that is, the devil;*"* and, with this end, we must surely infer without any risk of being wise above that is written, *Creation was subjected to vanity and the law of decay.* Otherwise it would not have been a world suitable either for fallen man or for the great acts of Redemption.

This, I say, is the inference which we might draw even from the Old Testament Scriptures. But the apostolic teaching makes this even more apparent. Thus St. Peter † reminds us that we were redeemed "with the precious blood of Christ, as of a lamb without blemish and without spot; who *verily was foreordained* (Gr. foreknown) *before the foundation of the world.*" And so St. John in the Apocalypse ‡ speaks of names "*written in the Book of Life of the Lamb that hath been slain from the foundation of the world.*" As also St. Paul § reminds us that God "*chose us in Christ before the foundation of the world.*" All this language distinctly implies that God's purposes in redemption itself, and in all the consequences of redemption, *preceded* creation: they were, so to speak, not an afterthought, as man is apt to think of them, but the result of counsels which anticipated all other works of the Eternal God. And this consideration—I mean, that Creation, though not in its manifestation in time, yet in the order of the Divine counsels, was subsequent to redemption—sufficiently explains, what otherwise might seem a difficulty, why St. Paul, having evidently in his thoughts the history in Genesis of the Fall and its consequences, connects it with the condition of ματαιότης, which is, by creation, that of all nature. Although

* Heb. ii. 14.   † 1 Peter i. 19, 20.
‡ Rev. xiii. 8, cf. xvii. 8.   § Ephes. i. 4.

in time this subjection was antecedent, in the mind of Him "who subjected it in hope," the order is reversed.

It may be asked, how is this original subjection of creation to vanity and a law of decay consistent with the words of the inspired history, "God saw everything that He had made, and behold it was very good"? But in fact it is the very goodness of creation in itself that makes its subjection to such a law of decay so grievous a burden, one under which all nature groans and travails with pain, earnestly looking forward to the time when its deliverance shall come. And were it not for the evil, moral and physical, that through the Fall tainted and changed the nature of man, even this earth itself might be a paradise, and an image to man of heaven; for, as indeed is indicated sufficiently in the history of the Fall, the change *consequent upon* the sin of man was not a change in God's creation, but in man's nature, which, having through his own will lost the supernatural gift of immortality, and all its accompanying blessings and enjoyments, needed now, for the continuance of this mortal life from day to day, a sustenance which was not before demanded by the same imperative necessity. The Septuagint translates the words which in our Authorized Version are rendered "Cursed is the ground for thy sake," by ἐπικατάρατος ἡ γῆ ἐν τοῖς ἔργοις σοῦ, "*in thy works.*" And again (as commentators notice), the sentence is, "Thorns and thistles shall it bring forth *to thee.*" And so Hooker* speaks of "the Divine malediction laid for the sin of man on those creatures which *God had made for the use of man.*" Indeed, that this was the true meaning of the curse on the earth for man's sin,—namely, that those elements in nature which might in the time of man's innocency have been harmless or even beneficial to man, became through his transgression

---

* "Eccles. Pol.," I. iii. 3.

a memorial and a chastisement for his sin,—was long since recognized by the sagacious and philosophic mind of Augustine. He says * of those words, "*Thorns and thistles shall it bring forth to thee,*" that we need not suppose ("non facile dicendum est,") that then for the first time these grew from the earth. Even in such plants there are useful properties, and therefore they might have had their own place in the economy of nature, without being in any way injurious to man. They might provide food for birds or for cattle, and be applied by man himself to some useful purposes. But when man was compelled, instead of refreshing his bodily frame by the spontaneous produce of the earth, to obtain the bread necessary to sustain life by the sweat of his brow, then these became causes of increased labour and difficulty to him, instead of serving their natural uses.† But interesting and instructive as is this exposition of St. Augustine, Holy Scripture itself carries on our thoughts much further in this direction. I mean, as indicating that it is the sin of man, and God's anger against sin, that makes nature as created by God, and the whole world, nothing but vanity to man. In the Book of Ecclesiastes, for example, the vanity of creation *in itself* is but the first note struck by the preacher; the general theme of the book is *the vanity of earthly things in man's use of them all;* because, though "God made man upright, they have sought out many inventions," ‡ and further, "because sentence against an evil work is not executed speedily, therefore the heart of the sons of men is fully set in them to do evil." § This sinful tendency in man, bringing forth fruits of bitterness in all the use of God's natural gifts and in all earthly relations, makes the whole of

---

* "De Gen. ad Lit." III., xviii.
† See Note K in Appendix.
‡ Eccles. vii. 29.   § Eccles. viii. 11.

human life, from childhood to the grave,—all pursuits in life, whether in a high estate or a low estate, whether the labour of the hands or the exercise of the intellectual powers,—vanity and vexation of spirit. The conclusion of this whole matter is : * " Fear God, and keep His commandments, for this is the whole man "—(as the words mean) : this alone in his whole life, in his whole being, in all the work of man upon earth, is not vanity. Again in the ninetieth Psalm, " Moses, the man of God," though he preaches, so to speak, from a different text, yet teaches the same lesson, dwelling more definitely on the vanity of human life as God's punishment on man for his sins, and as the necessary chastisement to bring man to true wisdom. He points us first to the Lord as the only *home*, the resting-place and shelter, for His people in all generations. Before creation, from ages past to endless ages to come, He is God : the same yesterday and for ever. But man's life, in consequence of the judgment of God upon his sin, is like nature; it is but a continual succession of death and birth; one generation passes away and another succeeds. He compares the life of man to the frailest and most perishable of nature's productions,—the grass of the field, that in the morning is green and flourishing, in the evening is cut down and withereth. The only satisfaction for the soul of man can be in the mercy of God, and the knowledge of His work and His glory. That will establish the work of our hands, and make our life not vanity and vexation of spirit, but joy and gladness all our days, and clothe us with the beauty of the Lord our God.

When we compare together these various aspects of the vanity of man's life on the earth, presented us in the Old Testament, we can have no difficulty in understanding why

* Eccles xii. 13.

in St. Paul's mind, as in the wisdom of Him who is the Eternal God, the condition of creation as in subjection to vanity and the bondage of the law of decay is connected with the punishment of man for his transgression of the law of his Creator.

St. Paul, however, reminds us also that this condition of creation is provisional. It is not the result of any moral evil in nature itself, as man's present condition is of sin in him; but it is ordained by God as being suitable for man's fallen state, until the time of redemption shall be fully accomplished. Nature and man are connected together in the temporary triumph of the evil, and they will be associated also in the final victory of the Son of Man and of His saints, when the promise of God by the prophet Isaiah shall be fulfilled: "*Behold, I create new heavens and a new earth; and the former shall not be remembered, nor come upon the heart.*" * This hope as to a creation that is to come, lies, of course, beyond the scope of this treatise, which discusses the Christian Faith on the subject of Creation as it now is. It has, however, a very important bearing on this latter question, because it enables us to explain how it is that while this present creation is the result of infinite goodness and almighty wisdom, it is yet, by its very constitution, subject to $\mu\alpha\tau\alpha\iota\acute{o}\tau\eta\varsigma$, to decay and death. We are not to suppose that this indicates either any want of power or goodness in the Creator; or, what seems to infidelity in the present day, as well as to Manichæism and other heresies of old, the only alternative, viz., the existence of an independent principle of evil in nature. On the contrary, it teaches us that the eternal and almighty wisdom by which all things were created, while it formed the earth to be inhabited by man, yet created it with a view to higher

* Isa. xv. 17.

purposes than those of the temporal and earthly interests of man.

How this part of the Christian Faith on the subject of Creation has been confirmed and illustrated through the progress of Science, we must consider in the second part of this treatise.* But its theological value—quite independently of the light it throws on such questions as those of "defects in the physical or organic world," and others discussed in works on Theism—is (one might have thought) sufficient to have directed to a subject, which treats of the profound relations between Creation and Redemption, more attention than it has hitherto received from theologians. And in substance, it really is, when we examine it, nothing else than the truth which we have all admitted, without perhaps recognizing its full force, that "the things which are seen are temporal; but the things which are not seen"—and only these—"are eternal."

* See Part II., chap. x.

PART II.

SCIENTIFIC ASPECTS OF CREATION.

CONTENTS OF PART II.

CHAP. I. SCIENCE INTERPRETS DIVINE WISDOM IN CREATION.
,, II. PRIMARY CREATION BEYOND SCIENCE.
,, III. LAW IN CREATION.
,, IV. IMMENSITY OF CREATION.
,, V. LIFE IN OTHER WORLDS.
,, VI. LAW OF EVOLUTION.
,, VII. EVOLUTION OF THE INORGANIC UNIVERSE.
,, VIII. ORGANIC NATURE.
,, IX. CREATION OF MAN.
,, X. LAW OF DECAY.
,, XI. CONCLUSION.

APPENDIX.

CHAPTER I.

SCIENCE INTERPRETS DIVINE WISDOM IN CREATION.

IT seems impossible not to infer from St. Paul's argument (Rom. i. 18, 19), as to the manifestation of the invisible things of God, ever since the creation of the world, through the things that are made, that in proportion as science is a faithful interpreter of nature, in that proportion will the manifestation of that which may be known of God through nature be distinct and conclusive. Those attributes of God which the apostle mentions, as especially exhibited in the works of creation, are *His everlasting power and His divinity.**
It must be noticed, however, that the word "power" here by no means excludes the idea of wisdom, but implies ability to effect that which is determined, by whatsoever means; and in this sense the highest form of power is wisdom; and this, as we have seen, is emphatically true of Divine Wisdom. The special force of the words here used by St. Paul seems to lie in the truth that the power exercised by God in His works is "*everlasting;*" it was not merely put forth for a time to call the present frame of nature into existence, but it is in perpetual operation, so that "the things that are made" are witnesses, not only to the power of the Almighty in that which is past, but also (and to those who have not the light of Revelation espe-

* ἥ τε ἀίδιος αὐτοῦ δύναμις καὶ θειότης.

cially) to His continual presence in the things that are made. And the other word, "divinity," expands that idea, so as to include all the perfections which are essential to the one, true, ever-living, ever-present God. These, he says, are so clearly to be seen in nature around us, that men are without excuse if they suppress their own knowledge of God, and through love of sin, and the bondage of their hearts and wills to the law of unrighteousness in their members, fail to glorify their Creator as God, and to be thankful to Him for His gifts in nature and providence.

It is indeed evident that the appeal which God's works make to man is not merely to his intellect, but to his conscience, which cannot fail to recognise God in those works unless it is darkened by the lusts of the flesh or the pride of the spirit; yet if science expounds nature truly to human reason, the result must be that the voice which testifies of God becomes more distinct and more emphatic, in proportion as it is more intelligible. For example, if the works of God in creation are a testimony to His unity, that there is but one God in heaven and earth, how greatly is that testimony confirmed by the discovery that science has made to us, of the unity of natural laws throughout the whole universe, so far as its observations can extend. I have elsewhere* pointed out, with reference to the relations between science and religion, that the very same principles of unity, order, and causation,—which science is compelled to postulate, without which science could not exist, which it therefore seeks in nature, and which, though it never can prove them to be universally true (since the range of its own knowledge of the universe is infinitesimally small, compared with all that is unknown), yet it does verify within that range,—are principles, of which

* In the Annual Address to the Victoria Institute, 1880.

Science interprets Divine Wisdom. 101

faith in God as the Creator of heaven and earth alone supplies a rational basis. It follows, therefore, that all the discoveries of science which illustrate and tend to establish these fundamental principles are additional testimonies to the one Author of nature, who is Infinite and Eternal.

This view of the aid that physical science, if she faithfully fulfils her legitimate functions, must render to faith in God as " Maker of heaven and earth," is of course both confirmed and enlarged by the truth, which we have fully discussed in the first part of this treatise, of the whole creation of God being the work of that Wisdom of which the reason of man is the reflection. Just so far as science is itself the result of *reason*, it must make manifest the wisdom no less than the power of God in His works.

And one cannot but feel that if the teaching of the New Testament—that without "the Word" was not anything made that has been made—had been, in modern times, as the discoveries of science advanced, more expressly and explicitly recognised by Christian teachers, the state of the question between Religion and Science might have been much more satisfactory than it actually is at the present hour. This incalculably precious truth of the Eternal Son being the first principle of the creation of God,* in Whom and through Whom all Creation was made, and conditioned, and subsists, is too often regarded (and that not merely by superficial readers of Holy Scripture, but by learned theologians and able and pious divines) rather as a dogma to be taught authoritatively, and believed implicitly,—an article of the faith revealed in Scripture,—than as a living truth, which expounds to us the relation of God's Wisdom with all the laws and operations of nature, and

* Rev. iii. 14 : ἡ ἀρχὴ τῆς κτίσεως τοῦ θεοῦ ; *cf.* Alford's note as to the force of ἀρχή.

with all the researches of man's reason into those laws and their results. Had this been recognised as it ought to have been recognised, theologians would surely have taken from the first a different attitude towards science. It is to be feared, indeed, that even to the present hour, notwithstanding all the profound, and no doubt logically conclusive, arguments by which it has been proved that there is no contradiction between science and Holy Scripture,—in spite of all these it is still tacitly assumed, *on both sides*, that even if from time to time a temporary peace may be made between them, physical science is, so to speak, the natural adversary of religious belief. This is the feeling, not only of many earnest if not well-informed Christians, but also of some who, though not theologians, but writing from the side of philosophy, yet apprehend that the Christian faith needs continual protection against the assaults of physical science. Sir William Hamilton, it is well known, argued that the study of natural science diverts the mind from the phenomena of moral liberty, and disqualifies the intellect for appreciating their import.* And further by habituating the mind to contemplate an order in which everything is determined by the laws of mechanical necessity, the result, he maintained, is that if the student of physical science speculates at all he must become a materialist. And he considered that the progress of physical science must necessarily increase the dangers of these atheistical tendencies, because, as science goes presumptuously forward, solving one mystery after another, and giving intelligible explanations fatal to all reverent feeling, the idea will become confirmed that as the mechanism of nature can explain so much, it must in time

* I quote from a review of the "Unseen Universe" in the *Church Quarterly Review*, in which I referred to these opinions of Sir W. Hamilton.

explain all. Without questioning that an exclusive devotion to the study of physical science is attended by some danger, and at all events may make the mind one-sided in its views of truth, yet it may be well doubted whether the progress of physical science in itself is attended by any of these perils.

But if such apprehension as to the danger to which faith is exposed from physical science could exist even in a philosophical mind, it is no wonder that alarms have been excited in ordinary Christian minds. On the other hand, the authors of the "Unseen Universe,"—by far the most important work that has appeared from the scientific side in modern times, as to the relations between Science and Faith,—write with the express purpose of reassuring "those somewhat over timid people" who fear that the progress of intellectual energy in the direction of physical discovery not merely has swept away some ancient fences and landmarks, but also threatens to engulf in its rising tide all the most precious hopes and interests of Christians. Their very purpose, as stated by themselves, seems to allow that these fears as to the results of such progress are not altogether without cause. But profoundly interesting as the speculations of that book undoubtedly are, to those who can appreciate its arguments, they are hardly such as can carry conviction home to the mind of an ordinary Christian who might be troubled with these apprehensions. To an earnest soul who feels the absolute necessity of a solid foundation for his faith, the question must surely suggest itself, whether that knowledge of God and of Jesus Christ, which is life eternal, can require, in order that its foundations may not be overthrown by the progress of physical science, the support of abstruse scientific theories, which, however probable as provisional hypotheses, yet certainly cannot be accepted as conclusions logically deduced from self-evident truth, and are not maintained as such by the authors themselves.

But might not the general relation between modern science and the faith of Christ's Church have been altogether of a different character, if the truth which is taught in Holy Scripture, as to the relation between Divine Wisdom and human reason, had been unreservedly and continually realized in Christian thought? It then would have been recognized that physical science, so long as it confines itself to those things that are within the province of Reason, is fulfilling the purpose with which God endued man with this great gift,—the first (we might almost say) of the characters of the image of God which man has received in his creation. So far as the discoveries of science are really the results of the rational faculty in man, they are discoveries of the exercise of the wisdom of God in creation, enabling us to discern, in whichever direction we look, the powerful action of that Wisdom. Far from supposing that true faith in the Creator is necessarily endangered by the ability that science possesses, or ever can acquire, of explaining as effects of natural causes those phenomena of nature which our forefathers regarded simply as proofs of the infinite power of God; we should rather thankfully welcome the progress of such triumphs of science as being additional evidences of the distinctively Christian truth, that in God's creation—being all effected by His Word—nothing whatever is made except through a Wisdom of which our reason is the very counterpart. The dangers on the side of science are: *first*, lest in the progress of science mere hypothetical theories should be taken for absolutely true discoveries, or (what is quite as misleading) for complete and final solutions; whereas, they only suggest new problems of greater complexity and difficulty. There is undoubtedly an illegitimate use of science when scientists abandon the patient and humble methods by which the real victories of science have been won, and again make the imagination the mistress instead of the handmaid. And when this error is committed by men of science, a *second* danger, even more serious, arises ; I mean, that science, or rather, not science itself, but a false philosophy using her name, presumes (as in a too well-known Address of a President of the British Association for the Advancement of Science) to enter into a sphere wholly beyond its own province and its own powers, and attempts to pervert the witness of nature to its Creator into evidence against Him.

But, however science may mistake her own office, or however inconsistent with reverence for religious truth the speculations of scientists may seem to us, certainly "in quietness and confidence is our strength." It is quite as necessary that theologians should confine themselves within their own sphere, as that men of science should do so. If we invade the province of science, we need not be surprised if scientific men trespass upon ours. Perhaps if theologians had refrained from those dogmatic assertions on scientific questions, which too often have excited, at the same time, the contempt and the hostility of men of science; and if we had, on the contrary, taught them by our example with what religious reverence man should pursue the study of physical science as the interpreter of Divine Wisdom in creation, by the careful and conscientious use of the Divine faculty which is the light of that Wisdom in our own minds ; we should not have had so much cause to complain, either of their substituting mere speculations for true scientific conclusions, or of their want of reverence in regard to questions of religion.

CHAPTER II.

PRIMARY CREATION BEYOND SCIENCE.

IT need hardly be said that to attempt to explain, in any forms of human thought, the incomprehensible mystery of the working of Him "Who calleth the things that are not as though they were;" and of the relation of the Infinite and Eternal Spirit with His material universe, is no part of the duty of one who would confirm others in the Christian faith. That God has created all things by His Word is a truth to be believed, not a theory to be understood. Faith can derive principles full of spiritual light and spiritual power from mysteries which it is utterly incapable of explaining. All that has been attempted in the first part of this treatise has been to clear away some of those false conceptions as to God's Creation which have arisen in the minds of men, from their interpreting language of Holy Scripture, isolated from and at variance with other teaching of Revelation, and according to the letter, not according to the spirit.

Although, however, we need not, in order to determine whether science aids our faith as regards creation, consider whether it assists us to understand the unfathomable mystery involved, it is necessary to examine the objection which is raised against the Christian doctrine on this ground by a certain school of scientific or philosophical

Primary Creation beyond Science. 107

writers. A late work of considerable ability, with the ambitious title of "The Creed of Science, Religious, Moral, and Social," discusses in its first chapter a subject which is generally supposed to be beyond the sphere of science, its title being "On Creation and God;" and if the contents of the chapter had been like those of another celebrated chapter, "There is No God in the Creed of Science," it might have been admitted that the chapter expressed an important truth, namely, that science deals with that knowledge only which is relative, and not with the absolute and unconditioned. But it seems as if with some writers the object is to represent Religious Truth not as beyond science, but as beneath it. The author begins by asserting that "the earth, the sun, and the worlds of space stand before us as existing facts, poised in space, and governed by law; and unless on the hypothesis of their eternal existence, as we now behold them,"—which he afterwards affirms, with sufficient reason, is a hypothesis which science negatives,— "they must have had an origin." And to the question, "What was their origin?" he asserts that "only three answers seem possible. They were created, or suddenly summoned into existence from nothing, by fiat of the Creator. They were slowly evolved by natural processes, such as are still in operation, from elementary matter. Lastly, the question is too transcendent for human capacity: we do not know; and we can never know from the necessary and eternal limitation of our faculties and means of knowledge."

We have already discussed the Christian faith on this subject sufficiently to understand,—first that it is no part of that faith that "*created*" means "*suddenly* summoned into existence;" unless it means that potential existence of which St. Augustine speaks in his exposition of creation, and (even so) in the Eternal Mind nothing is sudden; again, that it is part of that faith that all "natural processes" are as much the creation of God as the results of such processes are. It would be more correct, therefore, to have said that the only three answers that can be given may be classed as, (1) That given in the Christian faith, that the universe is created by God; (2) That given by Atheism, that nature was in its elementary matter self-existent, and in its actual form self-evolved; (3) The reply of Agnosticism, that the question cannot be answered.

The author's inaccurate treatment of the subject, however, is not our concern. That which requires notice, in reference to the argument of this treatise, is the following language in regard to creation, with which, or something of the same kind, we are all more or less familiar in the writings of a certain class of philosophers. "The hypothesis of creation in time need not be long considered, because *the thing itself is in fact unthinkable.* Creation *ex nihilo*, the creation of matter from pure nothing, is entirely unthinkable; while creation in the less proper sense of architectonic world-building from pre-existing materials, though not beyond the reach of a certain rude anthropomorphic imagination, is an unsatisfactory and inadequate explanation," etc. In support of his assertion that creation out of nothing is *unthinkable*, and that the hypothesis may be therefore summarily dismissed, the writer refers to Kant and Herbert Spencer. He has at all events studied the writings of the latter somewhat carelessly, and appears to have taken a passage isolated from Spencer's own discussion of the subject of the origin of the universe. Spencer himself says,* that "respecting the origin of the universe three verbally intelligible suppositions may be made. We

---

* "First Principles," pp. 30-35.

may assert that it is self-existent; or that it is self-created; or that it is created by an external agency. Which of these suppositions is most credible it is not needful here to inquire." He then proceeds to show that each one of them is "not even conceivable in the true sense of the word." He first shows that "The Atheistic theory of the eternal self-existence of any object of thought whatever is not only *absolutely unthinkable*, but even if thinkable would not be a solution." Again, "The hypothesis of self-creation, which practically amounts to what is called Pantheism, is similarly incapable of being represented in thought." For "to conceive self-creation is to conceive potential existence passing into actual existence by some inherent necessity; which we cannot do." . . . "This involves the idea of a change without a cause; a thing of which no idea is possible." In fact this hypothesis is, as we see on the least reflection, not only inconceivable, but that which involves a self-contradiction,—an effect without a cause.

That the third hypothesis, that of creation by external agency, is unthinkable, Spencer proves by showing that the existence of external agency is unthinkable, because it involves the idea of a self-existent Creator, which idea is itself inconceivable. This great philosophical discovery then, which is a reason why the hypothesis of creation may be dismissed without further consideration, amounts to this: that the self-existence of God is beyond the power of a finite mind to comprehend. Yet Spencer himself is careful to remind his readers, that which many entirely overlook, that "*it is not a question of probability or credibility, but of conceivability.*" However, the same men who will urge the inconceivability of creation,—that is, we find, of the existence of God,—as a reason for dismissing the idea as one of "no scientific or philosophical value," will assume, without noticing that their own hypothesis is open to the same objection of being unthinkable, the first of the suppositions mentioned by Spencer, as the basis of the Creed of Science. This author assumes the eternal self-existence of "a nebulous vapour diffused throughout space," "with a stock of potential energy," "subject to the law of gravitation and the law of the transformation of energy." The first article of the Creed with them seems to be,—"I believe in the Eternal Self-existing Ether, by the self-existing potencies of which the universe was evolved by the aid of the self-existent laws of gravitation and the transformation of energy." This article seems to include four inconceivable hypotheses, instead of the one contained in the first article of the Christian Faith!

But it is not, of course, on the ground of an hypothesis being unthinkable, or containing any number of mysteries, that there can be any objection to its forming part of the creed of science. Mr. Spencer has himself affirmed, that in the sense in which he uses the word all the fundamental scientific ideas—those of space and time, of matter, and motion, and force—are unthinkable; or, as he explains himself, "representatives of realities which cannot be fully comprehended." But it is a most transparent sophism to affirm that an hypothesis does not deserve consideration, and can be of no scientific or philosophical value, because it is inconceivable by the human mind. A treatise on the Dynamics of Nature which should begin by saying, "The Laws of Motion can be of no scientific value, since motion itself has been shown by Mr. Herbert Spencer to be absolutely unthinkable," would hardly be itself regarded as a valuable contribution to science.

Surely we need not be surprised if the idea which underlies the Christian faith on the subject of creation is "unthinkable," or, in religious language, "a mystery." It would be abundantly sufficient proof of its being incredible, if it were otherwise; if it professed to give, in forms of finite thought, an explanation of the method by which the universe originally came into existence. But although the author of the Creed of Science has certainly fallen into an error in his statement of the difficulty, whether we call it scientific, philosophical, or metaphysical,—for it might be considered in each of these aspects,—it must be remembered that there is a difficulty here, not arising merely from the idea of creation being unthinkable, but from the relation between the finite and the infinite, the conditioned and the unconditioned, the temporal and the eternal. In all nature, as its very name implies, there is continuity of natural causes and natural effects. All human science, with the exception of that elementary department of science which is nothing more than the classification of natural objects and phenomena, consists in tracing the continuity; and where it cannot discover the links of the sequences, it assumes them. But creation, in its primary sense, postulates a beginning to this chain of sequences, and therefore an original condition which has no natural cause preceding it. There is therefore a break in that law of continuity, which is, we have reason to believe, a universal law of all things subject to conditions of time and space.

But although this undoubtedly presents a difficulty to the human mind, yet the argument which is drawn from it against the Christian faith in regard to creation, proceeds on a fallacy, and is in fact a mere *petitio principii*. It is assumed that the creation of that which is material from that which is spiritual,—that is, *Primary* creation as distinguished from derivative,—cannot take place because it is not such a sequence of cause and effect as those which we find in nature itself; and though science may trace the law of continuity in the relation of the finite to the finite, of the law of the relation of the finite to the infinite, it knows nothing. To say that the law of continuity must always hold, is merely to affirm that there can be nothing except that which is finite; in other words, that there is no God. "Or to put the matter in another light. In supposing creation to be the first link in the chain of continuity, we necessarily suppose that, like the other links, it took place in time. There was a time before and a time after it. But time only came into existence when the creative process was completed. In fact, space and time, the laws of nature, and the law of continuity, are all relations of the finite world; and they could not possibly have any existence till the finite world itself existed : that is, till the creative act was completed. Hence, if we would grasp in thought the creative act (*i.e.* the *primary* creation), we must transcend the law of continuity; we must transcend all the laws of nature ; we must transcend and forget even space and time. We must view the finite world solely in relation to the Divine Intelligence of which it is the product." *

It will be observed how nearly the argument here resembles that which was quoted from St. Augustine's work on the history of creation in the Book of Genesis. It is indeed impossible, as is evident from the nature of the questions involved in the subject of the creation, to discuss them without entering into the sphere of metaphysical philosophy. For creation expresses, not only the relation of the finite to the infinite, but also the relation of Reason and Intelligence to the external world; and in its primary sense, as shown in the able sermon from which the above

---

* I quote from "The Christian Doctrine of Creation," a sermon by the Rev. D. Greig, preached in St. Mary's Cathedral, Edinburgh, 1880.

Primary Creation beyond Science. 113

extract is taken, is nothing else than the "externalization," the bringing into objective reality, of the Divine idea of the universe, both as it was in its original condition, and as evolved by all its developments in time. And there can be no doubt that this view of creation was to some extent recognized by Augustine* in some of the passages which were quoted.

It is, however, unnecessary to enter further into this aspect of the problem of creation, because the question which is discussed in this treatise has reference to physical science only. It is on this side that the chief difficulties on the subject of creation have arisen, and not on that of metaphysical philosophy. This philosophy, as a rule, has treated with much indifference, if not with contempt, the objection that scientists have raised in this field; and in Idealism it has proceeded beyond the teaching of Revelation itself as to the reality of things spiritual compared with those that are natural. And, on the other hand, English scientific thought has not generally regarded with much favour the speculations of this branch of philosophy. But it is a significant fact, and one that seems to indicate the possibility of important changes in the future treatment of the question of creation, that the necessity of abandoning, or, at all events, considerably modifying, the materialistic idea of the production of the visible universe, is now becoming apparent to men of science themselves. Professor Balfour Stewart, one of the authors of the "Unseen Universe,"—a work which to many seemed to err chiefly in the direction of substituting a sublimated materialism for that which is spiritual,—has lately, in a very interesting paper entitled "The Visible Universe; is it a Physical or Spiritual Production?" given not a few cogent reasons for

* See Note L in Appendix.

doubting whether this universe could have been produced, as physical science has assumed as to its development, by the mere action of physical causes on existing materials. It must be observed that the question is not as to the production of the material itself, the ὕλη; of this there can be no doubt, but as to the development. And although we may not be prepared to accept the hypothesis of the spiritual production of the visible universe from the unseen, as expounded by the author, without considerable modification; it is impossible not to admit that it removes some difficulties, which present themselves in the problem of the universe, of which the physical hypothesis can give no explanation.

In the meanwhile, though at present we may be content to wait for such further light on the subject of creation, both in its primary and in its secondary sense, as the higher philosophy may supply, it is an encouragement to know that all the mysteries of the operations of mind, no less certainly than those of physical causes, are included in that Wisdom of God, of which His Word, Who was made flesh, is the expression and exponent in His creation.

CHAPTER III.

LAW IN CREATION.

THE fundamental principle of modern physical science, as it has been (more or less) of all knowledge in every age which has been of the same character, is the idea of Law. To understand the relation, then, of science to the Christian faith on creation, the subject of Law, which touches both alike, must be first of all considered. Every theologian of the Anglican communion is familiar with the discussion of this subject in the First Book of Hooker's "Ecclesiastical Polity." His purpose, in that examination of the question of Law from its foundation, was very different from ours; but such an investigation is quite as necessary in order that we may ascertain how the Christian faith is affected by the progress of science, as it was in order to determine the true basis of the polity of the Church; and it is certain that, both on the theological and on the scientific side, the term "Law" is often used without sufficient consideration of its true force, and indeed sometimes in a very loose, inaccurate, and misleading way. Our enquiry will proceed of course on a very different line from that which was suitable for Hooker's discussion of the question, but it will deal with no less profound truths, and it may be well that both we ourselves and our readers should be reminded of the words with which he prefaces his examination of the subject of the Eternal Law.*

"Dangerous it were for the feeble brain of man to wade far into the doings of the Most High, whom although to know be life, and joy to make mention of His name; yet our soundest knowledge is to know that we know Him not as indeed He is, neither can know Him; and our safest eloquence concerning Him is our silence, when we confess in that confession that His glory is inexplicable, His greatness above our capacity and reach."

The Divine Law of which we have to speak, as affecting both science and faith, is that which includes all that are called Laws of Nature. Hooker points out, in reference to this Law,† that Moses in describing creation as the result of the word and command of God, had in view, not merely "to signify the infinite greatness of God's power by the easiness of His accomplishing such effects," but, "besides this, a further purpose, namely, first to teach that God did not work as a necessary but a voluntary agent, intending beforehand and decreeing with Himself that which did outwardly proceed from Him; secondly, to show that God did then institute a law natural to be observed by creatures, and therefore, according to the manner of laws, the institution thereof is described, as being established by solemn injunction." "And as it cometh to pass in a kingdom rightly ordered, that after a law is first published, it presently takes effect far and wide, all states framing themselves thereto; even so let us think it fareth in the natural course of the world: since the time that God did first proclaim the edicts of His law upon it, heaven and earth hath hearkened unto His voice, and their labour hath been to do His will."

* "Eccl. Pol.," I., ii., § 3.   † Book I., iii., 2.

This language no doubt Hooker himself did not intend to be taken literally. It was but in a figure,—though indeed he used the language of Scripture itself,—that he could speak of a decree being published and proclaimed throughout the universe, which Nature, God's creature, obeyed. But we must look more closely into this question, which in his days it had not become so necessary for Christian thought to examine, as it is in our days, when the progress of science forces it on our minds.

Now our previous comparison of the language of the Old Testament, which Hooker employs, with the teaching of the New Testament as to the office of the Logos, or active Reason of God, in creation, has taught us that the whole constitution and order of nature is the result, not only of the Will and the Power of God, but especially of His Wisdom. And it follows from this, that what Hooker calls the Divine Law, from which are derived the manifold subordinate laws of nature, as being its several expressions and applications, must be the Law of Divine and Eternal Wisdom. However, not Hooker only,—indeed his language is cautious on so profound a theme,—but, much more, theologians generally in our own day, speak of natural laws as differing, for example, from moral laws in this respect, that they are arbitrary, and such as may be altered at will. On the other hand, there is a profound conviction in the minds of some scientific men that the laws of nature are, like moral laws or mathematical conclusions from axioms, necessary laws; so that in their view it would be a self-contradiction for the Author of nature to alter His own laws in nature.

Although we must not presume to think that our finite mind can solve so abstruse a problem, yet the light which the New Testament throws on the subject may clear away some of its difficulties. The Christian faith teaches us that not only the results of creation, but also the causes through which those results are produced, and the laws according to which those causes operate, have their origin in the Divine Wisdom or Eternal Reason. This would be the case if the so-called laws of nature were so inherent in the constitution and very existence of that matter of which nature consists, that Reason, if it were able to know all the mysteries of nature, would recognize the laws as logically the effects of such constitution. The law of gravitation, in that case,—on the supposition that it is, as science assumes without being able to prove, an absolutely universal law, —would be to the Divine Mind as necessarily the result of the constitution of matter,—that is, of matter being what it is,—as the solution of a mathematical problem follows from the simplest axioms. The solution, complicated though it may be, could not possibly be anything else without the contradiction of self-evident truth. It is needless to say that it is not meant by this that finite reason could either so know the constitution of matter, or so trace the logical connexion, as to discover that it is a law of this kind; or even if it were, that the action of one such law may not be so modified by other laws of a different order, that to the human mind it might seem to be contradicted when it is not; as it is no contradiction of the law of gravitation that a plant grows up out of the ground, and a man can throw a stone into the air.

But besides this, it does not follow that because some physical laws are of this kind, all must be. Wisdom consists in choosing the means either necessary or most suitable for the highest ends. We have seen, in the last chapter of the First Part of this treatise, that the Eternal Wisdom of God had in view, in creation, other purposes than the interests of man's present life; and that therefore the present constitution of nature is subjected to "vanity," the law of decay, and is provisional, being a state of preparation for a higher, more perfect, and abiding form and constitution of created things. And from this it seems to follow, that in some respects the present laws of nature would also be provisional, and ordained by Wisdom itself with these higher ends in view. Even so in the religious history of mankind, the ethical laws given by God, during the preliminary and provisional economy, were not all necessary moral laws, although ordained by Divine Righteousness; but the Wisdom was manifested, not in the laws being the direct results of eternal principles of truth and righteousness, but in their tending ultimately to produce effects in accordance with those principles. And these subordinate and secondary laws were, Holy Scripture teaches, absorbed into the permanent and eternal Law of God, when their end was fulfilled. And may not this be equally the case in regard to physical laws during the present constitution of nature? This analogy may, at all events, remove some difficulties from Christian thought, although it will not of course obviate those which exist in the mind that regards nature itself as the only God of whom we have any knowledge.

However, so far as physical science is concerned, it does no doubt regard nature as governed by unchangeable laws; and all the hypotheses and conclusions of science must be formed on the postulate that they are immutable. And this teaching of science is of itself an aid to faith in God as the Creator. For no one can seriously doubt that a world governed by law is the only world suitable as a habitation for reasonable man. A world in which "chance," or rather confusion, reigned, and in which it would be impossible to calculate beforehand the result of such or such action, would only be suited for the abode of irrational beasts, if indeed for them. And this of itself is quite sufficient answer to objections (such as are raised by Mr. J. S. Mill) to the world being the creation of either an omnipotent or a benevolent Being, from the disastrous results which follow from breaches of the laws of nature. As Professor Flint truly says,* "The opinion that the world would be either physically or morally improved were gravitation to cease when men went by—were fire not always to burn, and were water occasionally to refuse to drown, were laws few, and miracles numerous, may safely be left to refute itself." It is indeed difficult to suppose such objections to natural law to be serious, or anything else than a rhetorical declamation, such as a writer for a prize essay might deliver against the enormities of civil and social law,—unless, indeed, we are rather to regard it as a passionate and irrational outburst of an antitheistic spirit.

The least serious reflection must convince any impartial mind that the immutability of natural laws, as taught by science, is not only highly beneficial to man, but absolutely necessary for the development and maturing of his rational faculties. And the fact of all these laws being ordained by that Divine Wisdom of which human reason is the reflection, opens a very interesting field for thought. All that practical science, which confers innumerable benefits on man, to some of which even the author of the Book of Job referred as known in his day, and which in our modern time have become developed and multiplied and extended beyond the utmost anticipations of the human mind, and to the increase of which there seems absolutely no limit,—

* "Theism," p. 416.

Law in Creation.

depends entirely, first on the certainty and exactness and uniformity of natural laws, and then on the power of the human mind to make itself acquainted with the operation and results of those laws, through man's own intelligence corresponding with the Divine Wisdom that ordered them. On the other hand, the rational faculties of man are not only cultivated and strengthened by the study of those laws, but the exercise of reason in any department of knowledge would be impossible, as far as we can perceive, in a world from which law was absent.

The importance of the subject of law to a right knowledge of the relations between science and faith makes it the more necessary that its meaning should be very distinctly apprehended. And there is an ambiguity in the popular use of the word in reference to scientific questions, which scientific men themselves sometimes overlook, and which is liable to mislead others very seriously. The proper use of the term *law*, in reference to any physical action of whatsoever kind, is simply the manner, measure, or order in which such action takes place, and does not include the motive cause. Thus the strict sense of the law of gravitation is that the mutual attraction of two masses takes place in proportion to their masses directly and inversely as the square of their distance from each other; the law of the transformation of energy determines the comparative amount of one form of energy when changed into another; the law of the conservation of energy affirms that, if by the application of any action to a body or system it is made to pass through any series of changes, and at last to return in all respects to its original state, the energy communicated to it during this series of operations is equal to that communicated by it to other bodies during the operation. In every conceivable case, "the law" properly means, *not the cause* of any change taking place, but *the order according to which* the motive cause acts, or the change is produced. And yet we find, in even scientific lexicons, *physical laws* defined as tendencies, determinations or affections of matter; and such inaccurate and really unscientific language confirms the popular notion that the laws of nature can be the *causes* of the phenomena of nature, whereas they only determine the manner in which the causes operate, or the effects take place.

Again, there is a distinction of much importance to be observed between those phenomenal uniformities which are popularly called laws of nature, and those dynamical laws, laws of force, or of the operation of energy, the truth of which may be verified to an unlimited extent by the science of mathematics, which is the science of pure reason. Thus, in astronomy, when the telescope enabled observers to make accurate calculations of the motions of the heavenly bodies, Kepler proved the existence of three great phenomenal laws which bear his name. First, that every planet moves in an orbit, which is an ellipse, the sun being in one of its foci; secondly, that equal areas are described in equal times by the same planet; and thirdly, that the time of the revolution of a planet round the sun has a fixed relation to its mean distance from the sun. But it must be observed that these, which were called laws, were nothing more than the systematized results of certain facts. *Such laws prove nothing beyond themselves.* They give no certainty as to anything that is not as yet observed, because they give no *reason* for the facts observed. But the true science of astronomy began when Newton, not merely by the discovery of the law of gravitation, but by the invention and use by him of a new mathematical process, determined that these phenomenal laws of Kepler were the necessary results of that dynamical law. The conclusions of astronomy are now conclusions of the highest order, because it is a dynamical science ; that is, one in which deductions can be drawn, through strictly logical processes, from laws of force or energy. Other sciences, such as those of light, heat, electricity, molecular action, have been in modern times gradually raised to this rank, and they are sciences in the true sense of the word, just so far as the phenomena observed can be interpreted by mathematical processes as results of a law of causation.

CHAPTER IV.

IMMENSITY OF CREATION.

BEFORE entering on the question of the light thrown by science on the creation of heaven and earth, in the sense of the *Genesis* of the universe, it is well that we should consider how the actual discoveries of science—that is, not conclusions from doubtful hypotheses, or inferences from partial induction, but the results of observation examined scientifically—have affected the forms of thought in which the human mind has embodied the teachings of Revelation on the subject of creation, in the sense of the universe itself which is created.

In all ages, the view of the heavens by night, with its countless hosts of stars, apparently dependent on the greater luminaries, the sun by day and the moon by night, was, to those who believed in God as the Infinite and Almighty Creator of heaven and earth, a never-failing theme for praise, and source of confidence in His power, His knowledge, and His wisdom. The stars which cannot be counted for multitude, and the sands upon the sea shore, were alike figures of the unlimited number of the promised seed.* The infinite knowledge of God is thus expressed by the Psalmist : † " He telleth the number of the stars ; He calleth them all by their names. Great is our Lord, and of great

---

* Gen. xv. 5 ; xxii. 17.   † Psalm cxlvii. 4, 5.

power: His understanding is infinite."* But nowhere is the feeling of the grandeur of this part of creation so strongly expressed as by David in the eighth Psalm; and the reference to that Psalm by the apostle in the Epistle to the Hebrews, definitely connects its language with a subject even higher than that of creation, the incarnation of the Eternal Son of God. "When," the Psalmist says, † "I consider Thy heavens, the work of Thy fingers, the moon and the stars which Thou hast ordained: what is man, that Thou art mindful of him, and the son of man, that Thou visitest him?"

As regards the idea of countless multitude, which Holy Scripture expresses, science, large as its discoveries have been, has only confirmed the idea by making it yet more definite; teaching us, for example, that most of the beautiful luminous clouds in the heaven consist of millions on millions of stars too distant to be distinguished separately by the naked eye. But as regards the *immensity* of this creation, and the insignificance of man and the world which is his habitation in comparison (so far, at least, as the physical *magnitude* of the earth and of the rest of the universe is concerned), science has given an interpretation which makes the words of the inspired Psalmist inexpressibly more forcible and emphatic. The first tremendous revolution in the human mind was, when the earth, which used to be considered as the great centre of the universe, was found to be only one of many planets moving in orbits round the sun. Then the calculations of the distances and magnitudes of the different bodies of the solar system discovered that the sun is considerably more than a million times as large as the earth, which is also far exceeded in magnitude by other planets of our system. The volume of Saturn alone is

* See also Isa. xl. 25, 26. † Vv. 3, 4.

about seven hundred times that of our globe, and instead of one satellite, one "moon to govern the night," it has eight satellites besides its rings. But the magnitudes and distances within the solar system, though even they are as practically "unthinkable" to the mind of man as infinity itself,—so far as the conception of extended space is concerned,—yet shrink into utter insignificance again when those are presented to the mind which are determined by the researches of science in the universe beyond. The fact is, that the magnitudes in the heavens convey no definite idea at all to the mind, except *as proportions*. "Thus," Mr. Proctor says,* "when we learn that a globe as large as our earth, suspended beside the moon, would seem to have a diameter exceeding her nearly four times, so that the globe would cover a space in the heavens about fourteen times as large as the moon covers, we form a just conception of the size of the moon as compared with the earth, though the mind cannot conceive such a body as the moon or the earth really is. When, in turn, we are told that if a globe as large as the earth, but glowing as brightly as the sun, were set beside the sun, it would look as a mere point of light, we not only learn to picture rightly to ourselves how largely the sun exceeds the earth, but also how enormous must be the real distance of the sun.

"Another step leads us to a standpoint whence we can form a correct estimate of the vast distance of the fixed stars; for we learn that so enormous is the distance of even the nearest fixed star, that compared with it the tremendous space separating the earth from the sun† sinks in turn into the merest point, so that if a globe as bright as the sun had the earth's orbit as a close-fitting girdle, then that glorious

* "Flowers of the Sky," pp. 20, 21.
† An error in the original here, apparently a misprint, is corrected.

Immensity of Creation.

orb—with a diameter of some 184 millions of miles—would look"—from the nearest fixed star—"very much smaller than such a globe as our earth would look at the sun's distance,—would, in fact, occupy but about one-fortieth part of the space in the sky" which the earth would occupy seen from the sun.

The fact that the distance of the nearest fixed star is such as is here represented,—which means that while light coming from the sun takes little more than eight minutes, light from that star would be more than seven years on its path, so that any changes in the star's place which are observed on the earth must have occurred more than seven years previously,—is of itself sufficient as a slight indication of the extent and, so to speak, the amount of the creation with which man is brought into comparison. But it may be well, in order that our idea may be somewhat more definite, to give another specimen (as it were) of this immensity.

There is a star (Sirius) which, though the most brilliant of all the fixed stars (as they are called, as compared with the planets of the solar system, whose motions are apparent), is yet by no means the nearest—but, as far as those distances have been as yet determined by astronomers, third in order of distance—that is, about a million times as far from us as we are from the sun.* At that distance this star only appears, through the very strongest glasses that have been invented, as a mere point of light without any disc, except one which is an optical effect. "But by comparing the amount of light received from him, with that which is received from our own sun, we can form tolerably safe conclusions as to the probable dimensions of the star. The rough average estimate that is formed

* Proctor's "Our Place among the Infinities." *A Giant Sun.*

from this as to the comparative magnitude of Sirius and our sun, is that the former exceeds the latter in volume *at least* 2,688 times,* and gives out 192 times as much light. Half a century ago, the supposition might have been maintained,—it was in fact suggested by so eminent a physicist as Dr. Whewell in his *Plurality of Worlds*,—that this star might be merely a brilliant light, and not an immense mass. But this idea, as regards either this or any other star, is now proved to be inadmissible. For such light energy is necessary, and for energy mass. And the science of spectrum analysis, which is one of the most important discoveries of the last half century, has given additional proof that a self-luminous star is a solid mass. It enables us by the spectroscope to discover important facts, both in the physical structure of the self-luminous bodies in the heavens, and in their chemical structure. It proves that all these bodies,—such as our sun, for example, —instead of being, as was formerly supposed probable, a dark body with a luminous atmosphere, must consist of an intensely brilliant central mass, surrounded by an atmosphere of comparatively cool gases, which produce, in the spectrum of the light coming from that source, lines which prove the presence in those gases of chemical elements which are known on this earth. Some of these elements are found by analysing the light from Sirius when it reaches us after a journey, say, of sixteen years. There is, I think, no discovery of modern science, not even the evidences of the law of gravitation holding in stellar

* I observe that Sir John Lubbock in his address gives a very much smaller number. I can only suppose that this, if not an accidental error, may be due to the consideration that the light of Sirius, as is possible and probable, may be *intrinsically* many times more bright than of the sun.

Immensity of Creation. 129

systems at distances from our system quite immeasurable, that gives us such a profound conviction of the unity of the whole created universe.

As regards Sirius itself, it need only be added, in order to aid us in realizing, yet more definitely, the unlimited vastness of the view astronomy opens to us, that there are also reasons to suppose, from the changes in the motion of Sirius, that the system in which he is the sun has non-luminous bodies, like the planets of our system in that respect, but unlike them in being not very much inferior to Sirius himself. If this is the case in one system of which from its comparative proximity we can obtain these glimpses of its superiority in magnitude to our own, while we yet find the traces of the very same creating power and wisdom, how immeasurably great must be the number of worlds, as large as these of our solar system or vastly larger, contained even in those regions of space the light from which reaches our earth. In fact, the idea of the extent of creation, while we attempt to grasp it in our thought, seems to overpower our mind. Certainly we must use David's words with a feeling of almost overwhelming awe: "Lord, *what* is man, that Thou art mindful of him; and the son of man, that Thou visitest him?"

But the question seems to be, does this marvellous discovery of science really aid faith by enlarging our sense of the goodness and condescension of the Creator? Or does it crush faith, by the enormous disproportion of the vastness of the material universe, with all these countless millions of worlds upon worlds, to this infinitesimal atom, the earth, which Revelation represents as the special object of the Creator's favour and love?

CHAPTER V.

LIFE IN OTHER WORLDS.

THE question with which our last chapter concludes was one which those who took an interest in scientific discoveries and their relation to religion more than half a century ago will remember was discussed with much earnestness at that time. It was in those days taken for granted by many Christians that all these innumerable worlds must have been created by God, as this earth was, in order to be the abode of rational beings like man.

In fact, as the Bishop of Durham observed, in the passage from his Newcastle Address which I took as a kind of text for this treatise, it was accounted almost a heresy to doubt this. It surely was impious (so Christians then argued), if not absurd, to suppose that these innumerable worlds would have been created at all, except for the purpose of being suitable abodes of life for those who might glorify and serve God as redeemed man is enabled to serve Him. The argument, as a religious argument, seemed incontrovertible; and preachers, especially those who were more scientifically disposed than their fellows, declaimed on the aid that science thus rendered to faith by opening to its view new and unlimited fields for considering the goodness and wisdom of God; while the redemption of the human race was illustrated by the mercy and compassion of a great monarch in sending the heir to the throne to a small distant province which had rebelled against its rightful sovereign, while all the rest of the empire remained loyal. However, there were probably not a few who felt that such representations of the universe of God were somewhat like arguing in a circle, when the purpose of the Almighty in these unexplored regions of space was first assumed; and then we were called to admire the power and wisdom of God in the fulfilment of the purpose. Besides which the feeling remained, that after all this did not seem to be exactly the position assigned to man in the revelation of the Son of God taking man's nature and dwelling among men on earth. The writer well recollects the relief given to his own mind, as his acquaintance with science was extended, and the discoveries of geology brought home the conviction, that we had been hitherto quite as much in error as regards the extent of *time* that had been occupied in the creation of the universe, as we were in respect of its magnitude and extent in *space*. The ages upon ages that appeared to be indicated by the successive geological formations, far from presenting new difficulties, seemed to be the solution of those that had before suggested themselves. For if the investigations into the structure of this earth teach us that the material structure of its interior must have occupied periods of years as countless as the stars themselves, even before the possibility of the existence of any form of life, vegetable or animal, on this globe; and again that other periods, equally inconceivably great, must have elapsed from the commencement of life on the earth to the beginning of the history of man; it does not at all follow that other worlds, even though they may be all ultimately intended to be abodes for rational beings, capable of loving and serving and glorifying God, have already attained that stage of their existence. It seems that after all, if the earth is but an infinitesimal atom compared with the rest of the material universe, the history of man also is but a moment compared with the ages upon ages before that history began; so that unless we have evidences, not only of the similarity of all these worlds to this earth in regard of their material and their structure, but also of their being suited for life, and further of their having become already the abode of intelligent and rational life,— even from the scientific point of view, the question of the apparent disproportion referred to above need not be considered at all. The language of the Psalmist, which regards with thankfulness and praise the condescension of God in selecting reasonable man, and this earth his abode, as the first and special object of His care and love,—as was manifested in due time by His sending His only-begotten Son to take upon Him the nature of man,— is in this view only confirmed and enforced by the teaching of science. The special love of God, in sending His Son into the world, is greatly illustrated and confirmed, without the aid of the proposition, either that other material worlds are the abode of spiritual beings (which was the idea of some), or that rational beings, with a material and fleshly nature, could, except through redemption, have continued unfallen. As regards the ultimate purposes of God as to the whole of His material creation, it is not for us to speculate.

Thoughts such as these were, no doubt, present to the minds of many when there appeared Dr. Whewell's well-known work on the *Plurality of Worlds*, the general belief on which subject he for the first time challenged from the scientific side. His argument, as against those urged by Dr. Chalmers, is stated with so much lucidity and force, as well as completeness, that although the later discoveries

Life in other Worlds. 133

of science have thrown much new light on the subject, which make some of the arguments urged on both sides irrelevant, yet it would be impossible to state the most weighty arguments more distinctly than in Whewell's own words.

He observes that the question which Chalmers supposes the opponent to propound as an objection to the Christian scheme is this:—" How is it consistent with the dignity, the impartiality, the comprehensiveness, the analogy of God's proceedings, that He should make so special and pre-eminent a provision for the salvation of the inhabitants of this earth, when there are such myriads of other worlds, all of which may require the like provision, and all of which have an equal claim to their Creator's care?"

Chalmers's reply to this objection is one drawn in the first instance from our ignorance. How can we know, from any information that science can supply, that other worlds have the like need as our own of a special provision for the rescue of their inhabitants from the consequences of the transgression of God's laws? "Since we know nothing about the inhabitants of Jupiter, true science requires that we say and suppose nothing about them; still more requires that we should not, on the ground of assumptions made with regard to them and other supposed groups of living creatures, *reject a belief founded on direct and positive proof, such as is the belief in the truths of Natural and Revealed Religion.*" But Chalmers wholly overlooked the fact, that in this reply to the argument as to the need of the inhabitants of other worlds of a provision for preservation from moral ruin, he himself was first of all assuming, without any information whatever from science, that such inhabitants exist.

"This appeal to our ignorance," Whewell observes, "is

the main feature in Chalmers' reasonings, so far as the argument on the one side or the other has reference to science. He indeed pursues the argument into other fields of speculation. . . . These he pursues at a considerable length, with great richness of imagination, and great eloquence. But the suppositions on which they are based are too loosely connected with science to make it safe for us to dwell upon them here. I conceive that the argument with which Chalmers thus deals" (that is, the objection before stated) "admits of answers drawn from modern science, which to many persons will seem more complete than that which is thus drawn from our ignorance." In other words, as Whewell puts it, that "*astronomy no more reveals to us extra terrestrial moral agents, than religion reveals to us extra terrestrial plans of Divine government.*"

Without referring to Dr. Whewell's other arguments as to the total absence of all scientific evidence in favour of the assumption made by Dr. Chalmers and his school, of the existence of rational and intelligent life throughout creation, it will be sufficient to give Whewell's philosophical and, so far as science then extended, complete statement of the argument from Geology.

"When," he says, "Geology tells us that the earth, which has been the seat of human life for a few thousand years only, has been the seat of animal life for myriads, it may be millions of years, she has a right to offer this as an answer to any difficulty that Astronomy, or the readers of astronomical books, may suggest, derived from the consideration that the earth, the seat of human life, is but one globe of a few thousand miles in diameter, among millions of other globes, at distances millions of times as great."

The author deals with the different aspects of the objection to the earth alone being the seat of rational life. "Is

Life in other Worlds.

it that it is unworthy of the greatness and majesty of God to bestow such peculiar care on so small a part of His creation ? But we know, from geology, that He has bestowed on this small part of creation, mankind, this special care; He has made *their period, though only for a moment in the ages of animal life, the only period of intelligence, morality, religion.*"

"Or is the objection this; that if we suppose the earth only to be occupied by rational inhabitants, all the other globes of the universe are wasted, turned to no purpose?" " But here again we have the like waste in the occupation of the earth. All its previous ages, its seas and continents, have been wasted "—as it is called—" upon mere brute life; often, so far as we can see, for myriads of years, upon the lowest, the least conscious forms of life; upon shellfish, corals, sponges." We are, in fact, not qualified to judge what may or may not be *waste* in the economy of God's creation.

"Or will the objection be made in this way; that such a peculiar dignity and importance given to the earth is contrary to the analogy of creation?" Since there are so many globes, similar to the earth, and planets of the same system, and so many other systems apparently similar to the solar system, is not such a general resemblance itself a ground for believing that the planets of our system, and those of other systems, are inhabited as the earth is? But, "if such an astronomical analogy be insisted on, we must again have recourse to geology, to see what such analogy is worth. And then we are led to reflect, that if men were to follow such analogies, we should be led to suppose that all the successive periods of the earth's history were occupied with life of the same order,—that as the earth in its present condition is the seat of an intelligent population, so must it have been in all former conditions." Whereas on the contrary the analogy utterly fails.

Nay, further, "the analogy points in the opposite direction,—not entire resemblance, but universal difference, is what we discover : . . . not uniformity and a fixed type of existences, but progression and a climax." Geology exhibits a gradual progression from ruder and more imperfect forms to higher types of animal life, until, after a long succession of ages, they reach their climax in man. How far these ages were *necessary* as a period of preparation of the earth as the habitation of man, or as a gradual progression towards the existence of man, does not affect the question. But the fact is certain, that man does actually form the climax, and is incomparably superior to all the preceding stages of the progression. "The analogy of nature, in this case at least, seems to be, *that there should be inferior, as well as superior, provinces, in the universe; and that the inferior may occupy an immensely larger portion of time than the superior;* why not then of space ? The intelligent part of creation is thrust into the compass of a few years in the course of myriads of ages ? Why not then into the compass of a few miles in the expanse of space ?" And further, if the earth was for ages a turbid abyss of lava and mud, and the germ of life were only gradually and at long intervals quickened in the terrestrial slime, "why may not other globes be still in these stages, or even in a condition incapable of being developed into such progressive states as our earth has passed through in order to become a suitable habitation for man ?"

The fact that man *is* the climax of creation in space as in time, and is, as a rational, moral, religious, and spiritual being, so infinitely superior to the rest of creation that he

Life in other Worlds.

is worthy of being the consummation of all this preparation, prolonged through countless ages, preliminary to his appearance, is a fact in itself which is the sufficient solution of all the difficulties which might otherwise seem to be involved in the limitations of his existence in the material universe, in regard both to space and to time.

It has appeared important to our argument in this treatise that the reasoning on this question by Dr. Whewell—who was unquestionably the physicist of the most philosophical mind and of the largest and most general attainments of all English scientific men at the beginning of this half-century—should be placed before our readers; and that not merely with reference to the particular point at issue between himself and Chalmers, Brewster, and others, but because the views he expounds throw a light on another very important scientific aspect of the great question of creation; which we shall have to consider in following chapters.

It only remains to notice more briefly how later discoveries have affected the question as to the existence of life in other worlds besides the earth. Since Whewell's time, two scientific discoveries have largely affected almost all departments of science,—the laws of "the transformation and conservation of energy," and the "spectrum analysis." There is no doubt that one tendency of these has been to confirm in the scientific mind the belief of the similarity, if not the identity, of nature throughout the universe. When we find, in the fixed stars, for example, by means of the spectroscope, some of the very same chemical elements as exist in our earth, it must strengthen the feeling that the constitution of nature cannot essentially differ throughout creation; and, if so, that the requirements of life in different worlds cannot very greatly vary, especially in regard to the *temperature* at which life is possible. The analysis of the light of the different stars has also confirmed the hypothesis that many of the chemical elements which are not capable of being resolved further, even by the heat at the surface of our sun, are resolved by the far more intense heat of other suns ; and in the light of some of the stars it seems only hydrogen is found. So that the heat of many of the stellar systems is probably indefinitely greater than that of our own solar system. On this subject Sir John Lubbock observes in his Address to the British Association at York in 1881 : "The composition of the stars (as determined by the spectroscope) is not uniform, and it would appear that they may be arranged in a few well-marked classes, indicating differences of temperature, or, in other words, of age. Some recent photographic spectra of stars obtained by Huggins go very far to justify this view." The connection between the temperature and the age arises, of course, from the fact of the lower temperature being caused by radiation of the heat into space ; but as the comparative cooling of the several bodies is a function not only of time but of the volume of each, Sir John Lubbock's language is not precisely accurate. It is, however, evident that now we must regard not merely the different planets and satellites of our own system, but also the various stellar systems themselves, as *in different stages of their existence.* In regard to our own system, there can be hardly any doubt that our nearest neighbour, the moon, is now in a state in which it is incapable of being an abode of any such life as exists on our globe,—or indeed of any organic life whatsoever. Through what stages it may have passed we have at present no sufficient means of knowing, except that if either air or water ever existed there, they have dis-

Life in other Worlds.

appeared; some conjecture that its seas may have been drained through the great fissures in its crust caused in its cooling. On the other hand, the condition of Mars and Venus seems to be so far similar to that of the Earth, that we may suppose them in somewhat the same stage of their cosmical life. While as regards Jupiter and Saturn, there seems some reason to believe that "both these planets" (I use Mr. Proctor's words) "are still passing through the fiery stages which belong to the youth of planet life." The "New Theory of Life in other Worlds" from which these words are taken,* explains, with the usual philosophic and impartial spirit of that writer, his own view on this interesting question, modified, as it has been, by the advanced science since Whewell's time.

He considers as probable some such view as the following :—

"Each planet according to its dimensions has a certain length of planetary life, the youth and age of which include the following eras: a sunlike state; a state like that of Jupiter and Saturn, when much heat but little light is evolved; a condition like that of our earth; and lastly the stage through which our moon is passing, which may be regarded as planetary decrepitude;" there being in all cases an enormous excess of the period when no life is possible over the period of habitability. "It is manifest that regarding the system as a whole, now one, now another planet,—or more generally, now one, now another member of the system,—would be the abode of life, the smaller and shorter-lived having their turn first, then larger and larger members, until life has existed upon the mightiest of the planets." But "the enormous excess of the lifeless gaps in our earth over the periods of habitability renders

* Published in 1875, in Essays entitled "Our Place among Infinities."

the conclusion all but certain that the lifeless gaps in the history of the solar system must last very much longer than the periods of life, in this or that planet, with which they would alternate."

Applying this to other systems in the universe similar to our own, we must conclude that "when we look at any one star, we may without improbability infer that *at that moment* that star is not supporting life in any one of the worlds that probably circle round it." But the reasoning which teaches us to regard every orb in space as having *its period* as an abode of life also "forces upon us the conclusion that among the millions on millions, nay, the millions of millions of suns which people space, millions have orbs circling round them, which are at this time the abodes of living creatures. If the chance is one in a thousand in the case of each particular star, then in the whole number (practically infinite) of stars, one in a thousand has life in the system which it rules over; and what is this but saying that millions of stars are life-supporting orbs? There is then an infinity of life around us, although we recognize infinity of time as well as infinity of space, as an attribute of the existence of life in the universe."

There can be no doubt, of course, that on Proctor's supposition of the number of the stars being so immensely great as to exceed, in an infinite degree, the average proportion of the lifeless period of a planet's existence to that in which it is the abode of life, his conclusion must be arithmetically correct. But conclusions from the science of probabilities are often very delusive. The conclusion first assumes that there is no unknown cause which makes the chances unequal. The chance of drawing a particular ball out of a thousand is arithmetically $\frac{1}{1000}$; but if it were marked it

Life in other Worlds. 141

might be certainty. And if there were any reason to believe that the solar system were the only one in the whole universe that had arrived at such a stage of its existence that any planet in its system could be the abode of life; for example, if every star the light of which could be examined, had fewer elements in it than the sun's light has: all this calculation on the ground of probabilities would be scientifically worthless. But, besides this, Mr. Proctor in his calculation tacitly makes an assumption, on which science gives us no certain information, viz., that the fact of a world being in that stage of its existence when it is capable of sustaining life, involves also the fact that life is called into existence during that stage. And this is an assumption quite as gratuitous, as that worlds must have been made for rational life. And further, in order to make this question of any importance as far as man is concerned, it must be assumed that a world into which life is introduced is one which in the period of its habitability becomes necessarily the abode of rational moral and spiritual life,—an assumption open neither to religion nor to true science itself.

But it is also evident, that whatever speculation as to life in other worlds may be probable or possible, this does not in the least affect the question of *our faith in a Creator;* and therefore does not touch the religious value of our belief as regards creation. The discoveries of science have undoubtedly tended greatly to exalt and enlarge our ideas of the greatness, majesty, and wisdom of the Creator; and (as St. Paul teaches us) of His everlasting power and His divinity. Science interprets to us, in the facts of creation which it reveals, a meaning, both in the infinity and in the eternity of the Creator, which the human mind could not have formed from mere words, however clearly and emphatically the ideas might be expressed in words. The only form of the Infinite, whether in time or space, that the human mind can conceive, is that it has no limit: but this idea is negative, not positive. The positive idea, however imperfect, can only be realized through comparison. And undoubtedly, the truths which science presents to our minds do impress in our thoughts ideas of the Infinite Creator such as we never could have conceived without the knowledge of them. They tell us of our own insignificance as compared with His works, and therefore of the incomparable value of being His children.

CHAPTER VI.

THE LAW OF EVOLUTION.

OUR readers will have observed in the last chapter, that it is not possible altogether to separate the view of creation, as a work of God now in existence, with the question of the *process* through which it was brought into its present form. This is the question which we must now consider at some length in reference to the enquiry, Does Science aid the Christian Faith as regards Creation? It will be remembered that in examining the teaching of the great Augustine as to the true import of that faith, we found that a particular illustration was used by him more than once, in order to exhibit the truth that forasmuch as all the causes and potencies which gradually developed nature into its ultimate form, originated in, and proceeded from, the Divine Mind, therefore the result of creation, whatever time the development might occupy, was no less truly God's than if He had effected that result by an immediate act of power. The illustration by which St. Augustine explained this, was that of the growth of a plant, with its leaves, flowers, and fruit, out of the seed.

It is certainly a very noticeable fact, whatever inference we may draw from it, that the very process in nature which Augustine selected to illustrate his solution of some of the difficulties in the history of creation, is the one which first suggested to the poet Goethe, at the close of the last century, that theory of growth or development which has been matured in the "Law of Evolution." I use the word "law" in its strictly scientific sense; for Evolution as a science deals *only* with the order of development, not with its causes, which may be and are very different, in different kinds of development. It is the more important on this subject to adhere closely to scientific exactness in regard to the term, because both on the scientific side and on the theological, half at least of the controversy has arisen from the illegitimate use of the terms employed. In this chapter, I shall confine myself exclusively to the investigation of the Law, as it is accepted in science.* I prefer to do this historically, rather than in the method which Herbert Spencer has adopted, quasi-scientifically; for whether or not his arguments are logical, at all events, both on the ground of science and philosophy, they have been assailed by many objections, and to many minds have not carried conviction.

The elementary principles of the science were, as I have said, first observed by Goethe in the growth of a plant, and they may be briefly stated as follows. When the elementary germ has begun to vegetate, separation ordinarily takes place into two rudimentary forms, the one representing the stem, the other the leaf; but it is not the leaf only into which the second rudiment is developed. All the other parts of the plant besides the stem, however diverse in

* I give in this and the three following chapters the substance, and sometimes the words, of arguments which were used by me in an article on Evolution in the *Church Quarterly Review* for April 1878. But the arguments are not only amplified as well as somewhat modified, but also in some very important respects very much extended, so as to present here a complete view of the whole subject as an aid to the Christian faith as regards creation.

The Law of Evolution. 145

shape and colour and size, are nothing else than different modifications of the same embryonic form, which may become either an ordinary leaf, or a bract, or one of the sepals of the calyx, or a petal of the corolla, or a stamen with its anthers, or one of the carpels, or divisions of the ovary in which the seed is formed. All these organs are nothing else than modifications of the same elementary form, transformed in its growth. The order of the transmutations must continue the same, but the process of transmutation may be arrested by circumstances during the gradual development, so as to prevent the maturity which is completed by the fructification from being attained. The existence of some such law of growth is indicated by that which all observers of nature must have noticed; namely, that in the same species of plants, the same number or some multiple of it is repeated in the different parts of the plant. But the proof of the law rests chiefly on the transformations which the parts of flowers undergo by alterations of nutriment and temperature, whether accidental, or applied artificially in order to produce them.

It is evident that some very important principles follow at once from the simple but very luminous fact of all these various parts of the plant being modifications of the same elementary form. First of all, the notion which was the original, and is perhaps the natural, idea of development, viz., that an infinitesimally small embryo of the matured form is contained in the germ, and that growth consists in the expansion of this embryo, is clearly shown to be erroneous; for the self-same part may ultimately become one form or another, the leaf or the petal, the stamen or the carpel, according to circumstances. Again, the causes of the successive transformations are of two kinds: those that are the primary causes belong to the original germ; others, that are secondary, to the environments, and other influences which promote, or prevent, or otherwise affect the normal development. Lastly, it is evident, that in this typical instance of development, from its first element to a complete organic whole, while it is true that the evolution takes place from first to last by infinitesimal changes, yet there are various distinctly marked stages and definitely separated forms produced in the process. The leaf once differentiated cannot be transformed into the petal, nor the petal into the stamen, nor the stamen into the carpel.

Although Goethe little knew how universal was the law to which his discovery pointed, yet he saw clearly that it was not an isolated fact which he had brought to light, but a principle of general application in organic life. In a work published at a later period he says:—" The *more imperfect* a being is, the more do its several parts *resemble each other*, and the more do these parts *resemble the whole*. The *more perfect* the being is, the *more dissimilar* are its parts. In the former case the parts are more or less a repetition of the whole; in the latter case they are totally unlike the whole. The more the parts resemble each other, the *less subordination* there is of one to the other. *Subordination of parts indicates high grade of organization.*"

The general principle indicated by the natural fact observed by Goethe, was subsequently enunciated by Von Baer, in the law that "development proceeds from the like to the unlike, from the general to the particular, from the homogeneous to the heterogeneous." It remained, however, for Mr. Herbert Spencer, in his " First Principles," the first edition of which was published little more than twenty years ago, to discuss this law fully, and to expand it into its complete form; the word "Evolution" being finally selected—although it is on many accounts, as he acknowledges, open to objection—as the scientific term for what had previously been understood by development. And, omitting that part of the law which does not affect the present question, we may give the definition in his words as follows :—*Evolution is an integration of matter, during which the matter passes from an indefinite, incoherent homogeneity, to a definite, coherent heterogeneity.* Thus the growth of the plant into its completed organic form is the final integration; it passes from a homogeneous state, such as the germ and the cellular tissue, through successive differentiations and integrations, at first very imperfectly either defined or coherent; but gradually becoming more and more of that character, until all the several parts are distinctly defined, and (however unlike), all related to one another according to a certain order, all belong to an organic whole, that is, a whole of which they are the constituent parts necessary to its perfection.

That the laws which are so beautifully illustrated and so readily observed in the growth of a vegetable organism, apply equally to animal life, became an accepted truth, even before they were scientifically formulated. In one instance, with which all are familiar, the growth of the chick in the egg of a bird, the meaning and truth of these laws is even more distinctly proved, from the fact of the process of evolution being confined within fixed limits, and development taking place without any increase either of size or weight, so that there can be no doubt as to the evolution consisting of the changes indicated. The homogeneous contents of the shell have merely become, through successive integrations and differentiations, transformed into the bones, flesh, nerves, feathers, etc., of the chick, which, as a whole, is the final integration in this stage of its existence. The *ovum* is at first a mere point of living jelly, a microscopic cell. This first grows into the germinal membrane, which is found, when examined by the microscope, to consist of cells all very similar to the original cell, which have indeed been produced from it by a succession of fissures. After incubation a third layer is added to the other two; and from these three layers,—which gradually absorb into themselves, and assimilate, all those elements of the different contents of the egg which are required and suitable for the purpose,—the whole is built up. Through this process, the formless masses gradually change into obscure rudiments of the future limbs and parts of the animal, and each becomes more distinctly defined, and more and more subdivided into its several forms, until the whole of the development possible in its present condition is completed, and the chick issues from its shell. Now it must be observed here, first of all, that the true theory of development is, as before observed, not that the original germ contains the organism of the future chick in a miniature form, of which some preternaturally powerful microscopes might discover faint traces, and that then these infinitesimally small lineaments would expand into visible dimensions through successive stages of development. In the words of Mr. H. Spencer, "it is proved that no germ, animal or vegetable, contains the slightest rudiment, trace, or indication of the future organism; and the microscope has shown us that the first process set up in every fertilized germ is a process of repeated divisions, ending in the production of a mass of cells, not one of which exhibits any special character." In this homogeneous mass changes take place, the separate portions becoming more and more unlike, the distinctions gradually becoming more defined, till the perfect form is matured, each part and organ of the perfect chick being a modification of some previous structure in the development, and the whole being united together in one complete organic whole, every part of which is dependent on every other, so that the absence of any part would be fatal, if not to the life, at all events, to the perfection of the animal.

And we must remember it is not otherwise with man himself,—so far as all that part of man is concerned, by which he is allied to the animal kingdom,—than with the chick which is produced from the egg. Man also is evolved, in his birth, from a structureless germ, according to the same law of development as that which we trace in the growth of the plant and of the bird. Evolution then, in the production of the physical organism of each individual of the human race, is a fact which it is impossible to question. We must here recognize Evolution simply as the order, according to which God makes each man, as regards his body, such as he is. And this is the view taken of the subject by one who lived, and thought, and wrote, ages before modern philosophers had dreamt of the laws of evolution; but who yet recognized the almighty power and the wisdom of God in the development of man in his mother's womb. "I will praise thee, for I am fearfully and wonderfully made; marvellous are Thy works, and that my soul knoweth right well. My substance was not hid from Thee, when I was made in secret, and curiously wrought (as) in the lowest parts of the earth. Thine eyes did see my unformed substance (a structureless germ); and in Thy book all (the parts) were written, in continuance (during days,—by a process of gradual evolution) they were fashioned, when as yet there was none of them" (Psalm cxxxix. 14-16). It must be noticed also, that this Evolution, so far from being regarded by the Psalmist as any evidence that God is not his Creator, supplies him with a convincing proof of His infinite wisdom and his Divine power.

Thus far then,—that is, as regards the development of every individual organism, whether vegetable or animal,—the scientific meaning of development is undoubtedly true. But must we infer that the law holds in reference to all true development in natural things? Without accepting the scientific reasonings (some of them certainly erroneous) on which Spencer bases his proof of the universal necessity of this law, it is impossible not to admit the accumulated force of the numerous illustrations, taken from almost every subject of human thought, with which he seeks to confirm the conclusion that the law is universal. I will select two from those departments of natural science which touch most directly on our subject, that of creation.

1. As regards the general system of the universe, it is evident from astronomical observations, so far as these supply us with any definite knowledge of objects so remote, that there have been, and perhaps are still, processes of concentration or integration. We find clusters of stars of all degrees of closeness, and nature in all stages of condensation. When we come to our own solar system, whatever theory as to its original condition may be accepted, the present result is that there are separate aggregated masses, each defined in form, and of various characters, combined in one system, like the connected members of one body, through their gravitation to the sun, the central mass. The satellites of a planet are linked with their primary into a balanced cluster; while the planets and their satellites form together with the sun a compound group of great complexity, and, so far as we can ascertain, of great variety.

2. The same law appears to be followed also in the composition and structure of the earth, which are examined

The Law of Evolution.

by geology and its kindred sciences. Geologists and mathematicians generally agree, that the earth must have been at first a mass of molten matter, and therefore homogeneous; but all that we know now of its condition, by observation, is, that whatever may be the state of the interior mass, the exterior is a comparatively thin crust composed of the different rocks and strata, which human science can examine, and of which human art can avail itself for the great benefit of man. Generally, the process through which these rocks and strata were formed (whatever the causes were through the operation of which the various crystalline and stratified rocks were produced), was a change from simplicity to a great complexity,—from a state in which there was one uniform material, to one in which there are thousands of different materials, as different from one another as granite from the diamond, as gold from clay. This change has been also, as geology shows, a very gradual progress towards this great complexity which we now observe—the number of strata being multiplied from age to age: and (to use Spencer's words) "the more recent being rendered highly complex by the mixture of materials which they contain. This heterogeneous structure has been greatly increased by the action of the earth's still molten nucleus on its envelope —whence have resulted not only a great variety of igneous rocks (plutonic, volcanic, metamorphic), but the tilting up of strata at all angles, the formation of faults and metallic veins, the production of endless dislocations and irregularities. Again, geologists teach us that the earth's surface has been growing more varied in elevation: that the most ancient mountain systems are smallest, and the Andes and Himalaya the more modern. As a consequence of this ceaseless multiplication of differences, we find that no considerable portion of the earth's exposed surface is like any other portion, either in contour or geologic structure, or in chemical composition; and that in most parts the surface changes from mile to mile, in all these characteristics."

But we now proceed to a more important question. St. Augustine, we have seen, used the illustration of the growth of a plant from its seed to represent the development of creation through the power of the Divine Word. Is there any reason to suppose that the law of evolution, the principles of which we have been considering, is, more or less, the *order* through which the work of creation was accomplished?

It is a very interesting and remarkable fact, view it as we may, that Haeckel, the most extreme of evolutionists (in the sense of believing in no causes of evolution beyond those belonging to matter), yet recognises in the Mosaic history of creation the order of this law of evolution. "Two great and fundamental ideas," he says,* "common also to the non-miraculous theory of development, meet us in the Mosaic history of creation, with surprising clearness and simplicity, in the idea of separation or differentiation, and the idea of progressive development or *perfecting*" (*integration* in Spencer's terminology). "Although Moses looks on the results of the great laws of organic development (which we shall later point out as the necessary conclusion of the doctrine of Descent) as the direct action of a constructive Creator, yet in his theory there lies hidden the ruling idea of a progressive development and a differentiation of the originally simple matter. We can therefore bestow our just and sincere admiration on the Jewish lawgiver's grand insight into nature, and his simple and natural hypothesis of creation, without discovering in it a so-called Divine revelation."

* "History of Creation," vol. i., p. 38.

The Law of Evolution. 153

Very candid and condescending no doubt in Professor Ernest Haeckel to confer his admiration on the Jewish law-giver. But at all events, such admiration makes two points very clear. First, that the opponents of the Christian faith have no right to argue that the Mosaic account of creation is inconsistent with evolution, when Haeckel himself finds it there. Secondly, that Christians themselves may surely believe that the hypothesis of evolution, *when it is confined within its scientific limits*, may not only be consistent with the scriptural history of creation, but even aid our faith in regard to creation. This has been for many years my own conviction, and in 1870, long before the publication in England of Haeckel's "History of Creation," in which his remarks on the Mosaic account of creation occur, I had observed (in a "Lecture on Progress," delivered in South Africa), that "in no department of human knowledge are those laws of progress or evolution, which Goethe traced in the growth of a plant, and which have only been definitely determined in our lifetime, more distinctly apparent or more completely exemplified, than in the first chapter of the Book of Genesis. That inspired record describes creation as a gradual evolution, through a series of progressive changes. The whole was without form and void, and the first result of creative power is to separate this homogeneous and formless mass into two distinct parts: the light is separated from the darkness : the waters above from the waters beneath: the earth and seas are collected into distinct masses and divided : then from the earth all the types of vegetable life are evolved into their complete and perfect forms in which they have the power of reproduction ; the heavenly universe is also divided into its various forms and systems ; from the waters proceed all its multifold forms of life, and the fowls of the air : from the earth all its living inhabitants are produced, every beast of the earth after his kind, and cattle after their kind, and every creeping thing after his kind; until at last, as the consummation of all this development of creation, man, the lord of all, comes forth, receiving from his Creator distinguishing gifts and powers, in which he is allied to God Himself." But it must be observed, that in the Mosaic history of creation, that which is described is evolution in its largest and most truly philosophical sense, and not merely that which Spencer describes and defines. For evolution, according to his definition, can only take place in the same subject or category; for example, it cannot begin in the category of quantity, and conclude in that of quality. He illustrates the law of evolution in the formation of the sidereal system, in the solar system, in the constitution of the earth, in the social system, in the growth of a vegetable organism, of an animal organism, of the human family, of language, of painting, of sculpture, of poetry, of music and other arts; in fact, of all things that are the subjects of human thought and knowledge; provided that the evolution is of the same, or in the same sphere, so that its different stages may be compared.

But his definition breaks down, and development cannot be continuous, wherever there is an interruption, a *metastasis* from one kind of evolution to another, in a totally different sphere. For example, even if that were to be allowed, which hitherto is destitute of any proof, viz., that inorganic matter could of itself give birth to life; still the transition from inorganic to organic matter could not be continuous evolution. Again, the transition from vegetable life to the animal, is transition, not evolution; and, whatever may be said to the contrary, the change from the intelligence of a dog or a monkey to the reason of man, is no evolution, but

The Law of Evolution. 155

a transition from a sphere confined to things earthly and finite, to the sphere of those things that are spiritual, infinite, and eternal, in which man is the image and likeness of God. *But the Divine evolution which creation is, includes all spheres from the lowest to the highest.*

It is well known that the sphere of creation in which the law of evolution has been especially traced, considered for the present simply as the *order* in which that department of knowledge may be classified, is that of the animal kingdom. Let us then consider for a while,—for it is both profoundly interesting and very instructive,—the kind of spectacle which the existing system of animal life actually presents to our view, and which faith expounds to us as God's creation. In this system the simplest forms are represented by a single elementary cell, possessing no organ of any kind that the microscope can discover, living either by imbibing fluid through their outer surface, or by absorbing solid substance into the homogeneous and gelatinous mass of which they are composed. In other forms again we discover simple organs for locomotion developed; while in some even of the protozoa we discover pulsations of the substance which seem to be the first beginnings of a circulating system. As we proceed to the radiates, we have the polypi, in some of which the differentiation of parts is so imperfect, that they may be minced up and each separate bit will form a separate animal, while the higher forms have a complicated muscular apparatus. As we pass from the animals of the lowest orders to those with a more developed organisation, the characteristics of evolution, according to its fundamental definition, become yet more apparent; the different parts are more and more unlike one another, each having a use and function proper to itself, which another part cannot fulfil, so as to be in the truest sense an organ. And the several parts are more and more defined; there are distinct bones, and these of the utmost variety of shape, yet so definitely marked and determined, that from its shape and size, an anatomist will discover to what animal it belonged. There is also a most elaborate nervous system through the whole frame, and every vital organ is a structure of marvellous complexity. At the same time the body is symmetrical, and has a unity which is not found in the lowest forms. But it is in the body of man that the law of progress attains its perfection. Compare, for example, the hand of man with the paw of any animal, even of that which in its general structure seems to approach man the most nearly, the anthropoid ape, and the characters of perfect development in the former are sufficiently obvious. Observe the variety in the human hand, the distinct definition of the joints and fingers, and, at the same time, the symmetry and expression—that is, the unity of idea—in the different parts of this wonderful organ, which next to the face is the most characteristic of humanity.

In this view of the animal kingdom as almost continuous links in the chain of an ascending scale of life, from a single cell to the most fully developed and perfectly organized animal, it is evident at first sight that there is a striking resemblance to the successive stages which we find in the development of each individual from its own rudimentary germ. But there are some marked differences also, sufficient to warn us against drawing hasty conclusions. For first of all the parallel fails in this respect, that whereas each form in the development of the growing germ is a stage towards a higher form, and nothing more; in the animal kingdom, on the contrary, each class of organisms, from the Protozoa to the Mammalia, is "self-contained," sufficient for its own purposes; not, like the embryo, with rudiments of organs to be developed in some higher stage, but with formations adapted to the wants of the class. In some of the elementary forms, there are proofs of adaptation to their particular environments quite as remarkable as any that we find in the higher orders of the animal kingdom.

And further, while the embryonic form is simply transitional, one which develops into the next stage, the animal organisms produce their own form, and no other, except in some singular cases of *alternate* generation. And this is obvious therefore, that the law of *hereditary transmission* to which we must have recourse, in order to account for the infinite varieties of animal forms that proceed from elementary germs, all alike structureless, and not one of which is distinguishable from any other, cannot *of itself* throw any light on the method by which the Creator evolved the animal kingdom, in all its manifold forms, from the lowest and simplest to the highest and most complicated.

It must be concluded, therefore, that the general view of the animal system, though it illustrates in a very interesting manner different stages in the order of evolution, yet *in itself does nothing more*. That this part of creation, the animal kingdom, was actually called into existence according to this law of order, we might indeed conclude to some extent from the fossilized remains of organic life preserved from the past ages, the order of which in the development of the structure of the earth, geology interprets to us. Undoubtedly the testimony of the rocks is, and ever must be, exceedingly imperfect. It seems almost impossible that the science of palæontology should ever throw light on the original forms of life, since the simplest and lowest organisms are so soft and perishable that they would leave "not a mark behind."* But imperfect as the geological record is, it nevertheless does exhibit changes in the

* Sir John Lubbock's Address, 1881.

character both of the fauna and the flora of the earth, from age to age, generally corresponding to the order of the law of evolution. However these changes may have been produced, no one who studies them can deny that they represent a kind of evolution through the ages which God "thoroughly furnished" by the agency of His Word. This "evolution" is not, however, any more than the "evolution" of a single plant is, the ascent upwards of a continuously inclining plane, but that of successive, though nearly related, stages of developed life. *Steps* are no less clearly marked in the progressive creation of animal life than in the animal kingdom at the present day.

That, however, which has most of all confirmed in the scientific mind the conviction that the development of the whole system of animal life has followed the order of the law of evolution, is the teaching of the science of embryology. Indeed, it seems impossible for any candid mind to deny that the conclusion to which the phenomena of organic development points is that evolution, not creation of a direct kind, is the universal process, since in the animal kingdom no special organ appears in any class without there being in some lower class a more elementary form from which it was differentiated. And embryology teaches this more emphatically. In the words of Mr. Lewes,* "Von Baer, who very properly corrected the exaggerations which had been put forth respecting the identity of embryonic forms with adult forms lower in the scale, who showed that the mammalian embryo never was a bird, a reptile, or a fish, nevertheless emphasized the fact that the mammalian embryo passes through all the lower typical forms; so much so that, except by their

* Quoted in my article on Evolution, *Church Quarterly Review*, April 1878.

size, it is impossible to distinguish the embryos of mammal, bird, lizard, or snake. 'In my collection,' he says, 'there are two little embryos which I have omitted to label, so that I am now quite incompetent to say to what class they belong. They may be lizards, they may be small birds, or very young mammals; so complete is the similarity in the mode of formation of the head and trunk. The extremities have not yet made their appearance. But even if they existed in the earliest stage, we should learn nothing from them, for the feet of lizards, mammals, and the wings of birds all arise from the same common form.' He sums up with his formula : ' The special type is always evolved from a more general type.'

"Such reminiscences of earlier forms are intelligible on the supposition that originally the later form was a modification of the earlier form, and that this modification is repeated ; or on the supposition that there was a similarity in the organic conditions, which similarity ceased at the point where the new form emerged. But on no hypothesis of creative plan are they intelligible."

Had Mr. Lewes confined himself to saying that these facts are intelligible only on the supposition of continuous derivation in the evolution of the animal kingdom, he would say no more than would be consistent with a firm belief in a " creative plan," and a Divine Creator. But unfortunately modern scientists have been too often provoked by modern theologians,—who have taken on themselves, like the ignorant man described by St. Augustine, to assume the office of interpreting nature,—to retaliate by invading the sphere of religion, of which they themselves are at least equally ignorant.

CHAPTER VII.

EVOLUTION OF THE INORGANIC UNIVERSE.

IT has been necessary, in order fully to exhibit the meaning of the *law* of evolution, as formulated in modern science, to illustrate it from organic life; but it must be remembered that the principle extends to the genesis of creation from the first, as St. Augustine teaches: the truth which he affirmed, and which all those Christians affirm who realize fully that God created all things by wisdom and not by power only, being that evolution, through causes of which God is the author, is itself *creation*. Indeed, it is somewhat strange that, even among the strictest literalists, there does not seem nowadays to be any objection to accept the scientific view of the constitution of inorganic nature having been evolved through the operation of physical causes. No one, at all events in the present day, considers it necessary to believe that the structure of the earth, the order and character of its rocks, its coal-fields, minerals, and soils, were produced in their present form by a special and isolated act of creation. Faith, at least intelligent faith, thankfully accepts the aid of science, as interpreting to us, so far as it may be able, how the Creator set all these things in order. It is evident, therefore, that it will clear the way for the examination of more difficult questions as to evolution, if we first of all consider the subject of the genesis of the inorganic and inanimate universe.

Evolution of the Inorganic Universe. 161

In order to enable science to investigate this subject, it supposes the primitive condition of the universe to be matter of an extremely attenuated nature diffused throughout space, without form or order, which was reduced to order by the attraction of every particle of matter to every other according to the law of gravitation,* and of the transformation and conservation of energy, such as they at present exist, and other physical forces or causes of motion.† It may easily be conceived how enormously complicated a problem this is which is presented to science; indeed, to a finite mind, it is, as we shall see hereafter, absolutely and necessarily indeterminate.

The scientific hypotheses on this subject may be classified as two. The first of these, known as the nebular theory, supposes the primæval atoms, under the attraction of gravitation, to have "congregated into groups, more or less close, and these again into larger and larger groups, until at length the original diffused matter became resolved into a number of rotating nebular masses of spherical form, of immense volume, and in a state of extreme heat from the previous shock of their atoms, and of their constituent parts." According to the nebular theory, these rotating spheres of vapour slowly cooled by radiation, in cooling contracted, in contracting acquired more rapid rotatory motion, in consequence of which, through the increased centrifugal force, huge rings of vapour were at length flung off from the equatorial regions of the spheres: which rings broke up into smaller spheres, and in these again the same process was repeated, so as to form at last the suns, planets, and

---

* The assumption that the primal ether was subject to the law of gravity is purely gratuitous. Until the atom was constituted, there is no reason to suppose that gravitation existed.

† Graham's "Creed of Science," Chapter I., § 2.

satellites. Into the question of the scientific objections to this hypothesis, which are not only considerable, but some apparently insuperable, it is unnecessary to enter. Some of these objections are removed by an improved statement of the theory in "The Unseen Universe," which seems to suggest, yet more distinctly, the impossibility of the present order of the universe being constituted by the agency of physical causes under the direction of physical laws alone.

The second and latest hypothesis is due to Sir William Thomson, who supposes the sun and its heat to have been produced by the fall together of its materials from a state of wide diffusion; this rush together "of the whole immense materials with prodigious velocities resulting, through the transformation of energy, in a vast development of heat in a condensed mass, which formed the sun." The earth, and other planets, and their satellites, were formed in like manner, but cooled more rapidly in inverse proportion to their masses. This hypothesis does not attempt to explain more than the actual present condition of the sun and earth and other bodies of our system; and certainly seems to demand the supposition of agencies and forces, to bring all these materials at once together, of which we know nothing. Both these theories, indeed, can be considered only as ingenious conjectures of first-rate mathematicians as to processes through which, in conformity with those laws of nature the action of which has been investigated, some parts of the development may be accounted for.

Whatever scientific theories as to the genesis of the universe may be more or less probable, we must not overlook some general considerations of the utmost importance on the subject of creation, which have been suggested by

Professor Jevons in his "Principles of Science."* A brief summary of these will aid us in bringing the whole question before our readers.

1. Though we may allow, as a supposition necessary for science to make, that a *perfect knowledge* of the state of the universe at any one time,—excluding interference by the action of voluntary agents,—would give also a perfect knowledge of every future condition of the universe; in other words, that science must proceed on the hypothesis of the action of physical causes being mechanical and necessary (for otherwise scientific inference is impossible); it must be remembered that this perfect knowledge is only possible to Infinite Intelligence; our knowledge must always remain at an infinite distance from this goal. First, we neither know all the matter that has been created, nor how it is all distributed. Secondly, we do not possess a perfect knowledge of the way in which the particles of matter will act on each other. We must know *all* the laws of nature, and *all* the existing agents acting according to these laws, before we can determine what will occur.

2. But, further, a law of nature—taking the word law in its popular and widest sense, as including the physical cause as well as the physical order of its operation—*can of itself determine nothing*. It is a law *plus* agents obeying it that produces results, "and it is no part of the law to govern or define the number and place of its own agents."

Even supposing that all matter when once distributed through space at the creation was thenceforth to act in an invariable manner without subsequent interference, the actual configuration of matter at any moment must have depended on the original *collocation*, and each of the unlimited number of particles might have been placed in an

* Vol. II., 431—440.

infinite number of different positions, and endued with any one of an infinite number of degrees of energy acting in any one of an infinitely infinite number of different directions. "The problem of creation was, then, what a mathematician would call an indeterminate problem, and it was indeterminate in an infinitely infinite number of ways." "Out of infinitely infinite choices which were open to the Creator, *that one choice must have been made which has yielded the universe as it is.*"

3. We must further consider what Jevons calls the "hierarchy of natural laws;" that is, the order and degrees in which, among the various natural forces, one gains the superiority over others, and may produce results altogether unexpected; and in regard to the limits to which this action and counteraction of various forces may extend, and modify what appear to *us* necessary laws of nature, our knowledge of nature can give us no certainty. "We have a very good theory of the conservation of energy, but the foremost physicists do not deny that there may possibly be forms of energy, neither kinetic nor potential, and therefore of unknown nature."

In reference to this, I have pointed out, in an address to the Victoria Institute, to which I have before referred,* that the comparative stability or instability of chemical combinations,—which is of the character that Jevons describes, and the results of which are, according to the present state of science, absolutely indeterminate, and seem likely ever to remain incalculable,—is alone sufficient to show how totally beyond the power of science it is to determine, even approximately, the processes through which the whole inorganic universe has been constituted.

Such general considerations as these, which have been

* See Address, pp. 20, 21.

Evolution of the Inorganic Universe. 165

urged with so much force by Jevons, combined with the fact that science neither has, nor appears capable of producing, any hypothesis that can claim to solve satisfactorily even a very small part of the problem of inanimate nature, need not lead us to question that the Creator did evolve this part of creation by means of causes not acting externally to nature, but in nature itself; but they do certainly prove the impossibility of excluding the *Will* of the Creator from any idea that science can enable us to conceive of the formation of the universe. Not because we question that natural causes produce their own proper effects, but because science shows us infinite room and space which nothing whatever except Will could occupy, so far as our reason can give us any information on the subject.

But there is a particular and even more suggestive conclusion, to which science points definitely; and it is this, that supposing the original condition of the universe to have been a homogeneous ether or attenuated nebulous vapour diffused through space, physical science cannot explain the complete development even of the inorganic part of the material universe through any forces known to itself.

Before, however, we consider further what this very important conclusion suggests, it will be well to examine the question of the formation of the material universe from another scientific aspect.

The subject of the constitution of matter itself is one that in modern times has received much attention. One theory, which is known by the name of Boscovich, supposes that what we call matter is nothing else than an aggregation of mere geometrical points (without parts or dimensions), which are *centres of force*. This hypothesis does indeed get rid of some of the difficulties of conceiving the constitution of matter; and it was accepted (to some extent at least) by so great an experimental philosopher as Faraday. But to the majority of the true leaders of physical science in the present day (those, I mean, who are not merely empirical or phenomenological scientists, but students of dynamical science), this theory appears to be nothing but* the embodiment of an over-refinement of speculation surrounded on almost all sides by the gravest difficulties. One of the chief difficulties is that it seems totally inconsistent with the first and, in the opinion of many physicists, the *one*, characteristic of matter, the property of mass or inertia. The idea also of forces, and those of an opposite kind, attraction and repulsion, ultimately emanating from a point without substance, is a conception which has nothing in nature to correspond with it. A centre of gravity in a material body is nothing more than a convenient mathematical fiction to determine the action of the resultant of all the force of gravity acting on every part of the body.

The most recent speculation as to the constitution of matter conceives of it as composed of atoms, not hard and solid and on that account indivisible, as they were imagined by the ancient philosophers, but rotatory rings of an incompressible frictionless fluid. The great value of this theory, and that which commends it strongly to all mathematical philosophers, is that it has not only been mathematically proved to be possible, but it also brings the constitution of matter into the sphere of true science by giving conditions which will enable science, as mathematical processes improve, to investigate its different properties.

* "Unseen Universe," Sixth Edition, p. 138.

Evolution of the Inorganic Universe. 167

It must be remembered, however, that this hypothesis of vortex atoms is only the very first step as to the constitution of matter. There are not a few persons, and those of some scientific knowledge of a certain kind, who confound the indivisible atom of which matter is composed on this hypothesis with the chemical atom, which is more correctly called a "*molecule.*" Of these molecules Clerk Maxwell says,* "We have been thus led by our study of visible things to a theory that they are made up of a finite number of parts or molecules, each of which has a definite mass and possesses other properties. The molecules of the same (chemical) substance are all exactly alike, but different from those of other substances. There is not a regular gradation in the mass of molecules from that of hydrogen, which is the least of those known to us, to that of bismuth; but they all fall into a limited number of classes or species, the individuals of each species being exactly similar to each other, and no intermediate links are found to connect one species with another by a uniform gradation." He further observes that there seems here a certain resemblance to the different species of organic nature. But there is this wide difference, that whereas in the species of vegetable and animal nature variations occur, and there is a perpetual generation and destruction of the individuals of which the species consist, "in the case of the molecules each individual is permanent; there is no generation or destruction, and no variation, or rather difference, between the individuals of each species. Hence the kind of speculation with which we have become so familiar under the name of theories of evolution is quite inapplicable to the case of molecules."

This truth the same profoundly philosophical scientist

* "Theory of Heat," p. 330.

expressed more fully in his Address at the meeting of the British Association in 1873.

Having given the proofs that throughout the universe, and in all ages, the molecules of the same substance have ever been the same, he continues—

"No theory of evolution can be formed to account for the similarity of the molecules, for evolution necessarily implies continuous change, and the molecule is incapable of growth or decay, of generation or destruction.

"None of the processes of nature, since the time when nature began, have produced the slightest difference in the properties of any molecule. We are, therefore, unable to ascribe either the existence of the molecules or the identity of their properties to the operation of any of the causes which we call natural.

"On the other hand, the exact equality of each molecule to all others of the same kind gives it, as Sir John Herschel has well said, the essential character of a *manufactured article*, and precludes the idea of its being eternal and self-existent.

"In tracing back the history of matter, science is arrested when she assures herself, on the one hand, that the molecule has been made; on the other, that it has not been made by any of the processes we call natural."*

So far as we can judge, the molecules differ from one another solely in being congregations, differently arranged and constituted, of the same elementary atoms. And it has been said that a molecule of iron, for example, must itself be a vastly more complicated structure than the whole solar system. If such a view be true, the physical difference of the several molecules must consist only in the relative distance and *vis viva* of each atom of which it is

* But see note p. 173, at the close of this chapter.

composed. "The number of material atoms in each kind of molecule cannot be absolutely determined, so that our knowledge of this subject can only be relative to an adopted standard of unity; and as hydrogen is the lightest of all the elements, it has been more generally accepted than any other, as the unit of chemical equivalents. It was thought, at one time, that the weight of every element was a simple multiple of hydrogen; but more accurate analyses made it necessary to express the weights of the elements in decimal fractions, as in the following examples. Thus hydrogen being unity 1·000, carbon is 11·970, nitrogen 14·010, oxygen 15·960, sulphur 31·980, chlorine 35·360, and so up to the highest, bismuth, 207·500. Now if it be assumed that the molecule of hydrogen is composed of 1,000 ethereal atoms, then deleting the decimal point in the above notations," we have a conjectural number of "atoms in the molecule of each kind of element. And we thus get rid of the notion which is now so prevalent, that the elements are atoms and their compounds molecules; for the material basis of every chemical substance, whether simple or compound, is a molecule or little mass of material atoms. By admitting (says Sir John Herschel) that the particles (molecules) of bodies consist not of a few only but of a great multitude of thousands, or perhaps millions of atoms, not only may the facts of crystallography be represented, but much light also thrown upon many points in the theory of the absorption of light, the colours of bodies, and their power of conducting heat."*

Clerk Maxwell speaks of the chemical molecules as "the foundation stones of the material universe" which remain unbroken and unworn, whatever catastrophes may occur in the course of ages, though ancient systems may be dissolved and new systems built out of their ruins. And this

* "Evolution and Creation," by Dr. H. S. Boase, p. 75.

description of the molecules is not merely figurative, for they have not only weight but volume and form; as is indicated by the definite forms of various crystals of different chemical elements, so that there is reason to think that the molecule* is "the whole crystal writ small." The view, however, of these molecules being foundation stones that must remain unbroken whatever catastrophes must occur in the heavens seems hardly confirmed by the progress of science; since there is increasing reason to believe that the chemical elements themselves are in reality composite structures, and that higher temperatures than those now at our disposal might enable us to decompose many which at present appear to be simple. In fact, that sufficient heat might decompose all.† At all events, even scientifically, it is, as is observed in the "Unseen Universe," a speculation which ought not to be summarily dismissed, but should be retained as a working hypothesis which may in time throw great light on the ultimate constitution of the chemical elements.

But, without entering into this question, that which meets us at once in the formation of the inorganic universe is the inquiry as to the *results* of the chemical combinations of which its various materials are composed; and here we find immediately that physical science is altogether and, as far as we can see, hopelessly, at a loss to explain the properties of these results,—indeed, the properties of the separate elements themselves. Why the chemical combination of oxygen and hydrogen in the proportion

---

* G. H. Lewes, quoted by Dr. Boase.

† Is it fanciful (the question is asked by the authors of "The Unseen Universe") to suppose that the passage (2 Peter iii. 10) may refer to this, which says that in the day of the Lord *the elements shall be dissolved with fervent heat?*

Evolution of the Inorganic Universe. 171

of one molecule of the former to two of the latter should produce water with its well-known properties, so precious as one of the constituents of the material universe; this fact, common and simple as it is, is itself a mystery of which physical science does not yet possess the key. While of the strange, and apparently contradictory, properties of the different combinations of the very same chemical elements in different proportions, of the allotropic form of some elements, and generally of the whole subject of chemical affinity,—science can do hardly anything as yet but observe and classify phenomena.

When we take into consideration the fact of so many of the chemical elements known on the earth being discovered in some of the stars, while other stars contain fewer, and some of the whitest and brightest apparently only hydrogen, we may, at all events, suppose with some reason, that the primary steps in the creation of the *material* of the universe were, first the formation of the atoms out of the structureless ether that pervaded space, then that of the chemical molecules, as the heat of the bodies into which the atoms were congregated radiated into space; the number of the elementary chemical molecules increasing as the heat gradually diminished.

We have now, I think, sufficient information as to the development, both of the morphology (if I may so use this word) and of the hylology (if I may invent this term) of the inorganic universe, to venture to turn the negative conclusion* to a yet more important and yet more definite positive conclusion.

I may, I suppose, assume it as certain that with these facts before us,—on the one hand, of the orderly, though not uniform, distribution of matter through space in the solar

* *Supra, p.* 165.

and stellar systems, in regard to part of which science can conclude, both from the forms and the motions of the bodies,—so far as ascertained,—that it has taken place in accordance with the law of gravitation; and, on the other hand, of the material of these various bodies, composed, so far as known, of chemical elements and their combinations, and of mixtures of these combinations, the chemical elements and the chemical combinations being in the highest degree definite, the former throughout the universe;—no student of science in the present day, however disinclined he might be to recognise design in creation, would consider it scientific to follow "the natural philosophy of Democritus," and "attribute the form" of the universe "able to maintain itself, *to infinite essays or proofs of nature which they term fortune.*" Bacon* might in his day suppose this possible, and even more probable than that nature should have respect to final causes; but since the Newtonian philosophy, no one who has any idea of science could suppose that it was by such a method that the solar system has been formed and maintained.

But if we dismiss the philosophy of Democritus (at least as thus described, for it seems doubtful whether he does not mean by τύχη something very different† from our notion of "fortune"), the only conclusion to which science points seems to be the following,—and it is one the importance of which it is difficult to over-estimate.

The original condition of the universe having been a homogeneous structureless ether diffused uniformly throughout space, the inorganic material universe was produced by the matter passing, both as regards its external forms and its internal

---

* "Of the Advancement of Learning," Book II. (vol. i., p. 106, ed. 1824).

† Cf. Article on Democritus, in Smith's "Biographical Dictionary."

Evolution of the Inorganic Universe.

*structure, from an indefinite incoherent homogeneity to a definite and coherent heterogeneity, through the agency of causes of which some and their laws are partially known to science, and others altogether unknown.**

Such is the conclusion to which science directs us. The Christian faith has only to add,—that which it is its office to teach,—that all these causes, whether known or unknown, originate in and are maintained by the Almighty Power, the Infinite Wisdom, and the Energizing Spirit of the Divine Creator. And surely the aid that science thus renders to faith in regard to creation, by making belief more distinct and more reasonable, is not aid that should be despised.

---

* I am afraid that in this definition it may seem presumptuous to differ from the view of so eminent an authority as Clerk Maxwell on the subject of the molecules : inasmuch as the definition implies that the causes, through which all the changes were produced, were, or at all events may have been, physical ; whereas Maxwell says (p. 168 *supra*), that science assures itself that the molecule " has not been made by any of the processes which we call natural." He seems to consider them as having been made by the immediate Will of God, as part of the original ὕλη of which the universe was made. But if it is the fact, as is now very generally supposed, that many of the chemical molecules which are not decomposable under the conditions of this globe or of the sun, do not exist in systems of a much higher temperature, it is impossible not to allow that elements which physical causes can dissolve, physical causes also may have been the agents in combining. The fact that the development of the molecules was not *continuous*, does not affect the question. Many of the integrations of nature are not continuous, *e.g.*, that of the compound molecules both of inorganic and organic chemistry. Many such molecules (which human skill is incapable of producing) are produced in the growth of vegetable and animal organisms; which growth in this respect, as in so many others, is the exact counterpart of the evolution of the visible universe.

CHAPTER VIII.

ORGANIC NATURE.

IT has been indicated before * that Mr. Spencer's definition of evolution throws no light on the transition from inorganic matter to organic, from death to life. This becomes yet more apparent when we examine more closely the character of the change. Agassiz † pointed out that living forms are in this respect entirely distinct from those which are produced from purely physical causes, that "the products of what are commonly called physical agents are everywhere the same" (from the same causes), "and have always been the same; while organized beings are everywhere different, and have differed in all ages; between two such series of phenomena there can be no causal or genetic connexion." For example, all chemical elements and combinations are the same, and always must be: in the kingdom of organic life there is endless and constant variety. The whole character of the operations in the one class differs from that in the other. A production in the one cannot become a production in the other by successive differentiations and integrations; they are incommensurable. But Professor Huxley in his article on "Biology" in the ninth edition of the "Encyclo-

---

* Chap. vi., p. 154.
† See Jevons' "Principles of Science," vol. ii., p. 462.

pædia Britannica," makes this yet more clear.* He observes that the phenomena characteristic of living matter are strongly marked off from all other phenomena. Certain properties distinguish it *absolutely* from all other kinds of matter; "*our present stock of knowledge furnishing no kind of link between that which is living and that which is not.*" These properties are, first, the chemical constitution of living matter, as it always contains a particular compound of carbon, water, and nitrogen. The second is its universal disintegration and waste by oxidation, and its re-integration, not by external accretion, but by introsusception of fresh and suitable material, which in the animal must always be productions of organic nature. The third is its capacity of undergoing cyclical changes, the individual form after certain changes ceasing to possess the properties of living matter, but continuing and multiplying its existence, by its seeds or other living portions of itself, which in their turn undergo the same changes. Besides these properties, organization or the possession of special instruments for special purposes is usually characteristic of these existences. And to these it must be added, that in animated nature alone is any existence found, which though composed of different molecules, not combined chemically, is yet one individual.

For the present there is no doubt that the theory of spontaneous generation under the present circumstances of the earth's existence, as the explanation of the introduction of life into the creation, has received no confirmation. In a well known address delivered a few years ago, †
Professor Virchow, who has himself contributed largely

* See Address to Victoria Institute, 1880, pp. 8, 9.
† Page 36 of that Address quoted in the Review on Evolution in the *Church Quarterly.*

to the science of evolution, and who can speak with an authority that none would question, affirms emphatically, that "all really scientific knowledge respecting the beginning of life has followed a course exactly contrary" to this theory. He says further, "The *generatio æquivoca*, which has been so often contested and so often contradicted, is nevertheless always meeting us afresh. To be sure, we know not a single *positive fact* to prove that a *generatio æquivoca* has ever been made, that there has ever been procreation in this way; that inorganic masses —such as the firm of Carbon and Co.—have ever spontaneously developed themselves into organic masses. Nevertheless, I grant that if any one is *determined* to form for himself an *idea* of how the first organic being *could* come into existence of itself, nothing further is left than to go back to spontaneous generation. Thus much is evident. If I do not choose to accept a theory of creation; if I refuse to believe that there was a special Creator who took the clod of earth and breathed into it the breath of life; if I prefer to make for myself a verse after my own fashion (in the place of the verse in Genesis); then I must make it in the sense of *generatio æquivoca*. *Tertium non datur.* No alternative remains when once we say, 'I do not accept the creation, but I *will* have an explanation.' Whoever takes up that first position must go on to the second position and say, '*Ergo*, I assume the *generatio æquivoca*.' But of this we do not possess any actual proof. No one has ever seen a *generatio æquivoca* really effected, and whoever supposes that it has occurred is contradicted by the naturalist, and not merely by the theologian. . . . . If we would speak frankly we must admit that naturalists may well have some little sympathy with *generatio æquivoca*. If it were capable of proof it

Organic Nature. 177

would be indeed beautiful! But we must acknowledge it has not been yet proved. The proofs of it are still wanting. If, however, any proof should be successful, we would give in our adhesion. But even then it must first be settled to what extent the *generatio æquivoca* is admissible. We should have to proceed quietly to the investigation; for no one would think of maintaining that spontaneous generation at all accounts for the whole number of organic beings. It may possibly hold good only for one series of beings. But my opinion is that we have time to wait for the proof. Whoever recalls to mind the lamentable failure of all the attempts made very recently to discover a decided support for the *generatio æquivoca* in the lower forms of transition from the inorganic to the organic world, will feel it doubly serious to demand that this theory, so utterly discredited, should be in any way accepted as the basis of all our views of life. I may assume that the history of the Bathybius is pretty well known to all educated persons, and with the Bathybius the hope has once more subsided that the *generatio æquivoca* may be capable of proof."

It must not be forgotten, that in addition to this negative testimony to which Virchow refers, the whole tendency of physical science (in the true sense of the word, as deducing conclusions from dynamical laws) is in the direction of *cashiering* the atom (in Cudworth's quaint but very expressive language) of all properties beyond mass and motion; to which conclusion it might be easily shown that the properties of the combination of the atom in the chemical molecule are not contradictory, inexplicable as they undoubtedly are.

However, to all these conclusions of science it is very easy for those who are resolved to believe in life being a natural production of death, to reply that no experiments of a negative character have been or ever can be exhaustive. "The experiments," such men say,* "do not exclude the possibility that nature in her vast laboratory can and does at present evolve living from non-living matter; far less do they destroy the grounds of the scientific (?) conviction, that nature, *working under wholly different and more favourable conditions in the past, when the earth, cooling from her originally incandescent state, was warmer, and when her own plastic powers were greater, could evolve life spontaneously from her own breast.*" One is disposed to enquire what are the scientific *grounds* for such a "conviction," and what the writer knows of plastic powers being such as would quicken a dead mass into living matter. It soon transpires, however, what are the author's grounds for believing in spontaneous generation in the absence of all evidence. "The strongest of all arguments for the theory of spontaneous generation is the inadmissibility of the only rival hypothesis. In no other way can the origin of life *be conceived*, argues Haeckel. If nature did not evolve spontaneously the few primordial forms of life which the Darwinian theory postulates, then they must have been supernaturally created." The ground, then, for the "scientific conviction" is that otherwise it would be necessary to believe in a Creator.† He prefers believing in Haeckel and Darwin.

I am, however, writing for those who do believe in a Creator, whose spirit is the Author and Giver of life. And I may remind them that it cannot be "*scientific*" to disbelieve that which is inconceivable by the human mind, when, as Herbert Spencer we have seen contends,‡ all the

* Graham's "Creed of Science," p. 20.
† See *supra*, chap. ii., p. 109.
‡ *Ibid*, 110.

Organic Nature. 179

fundamental principles of science are of that character. And further it may be useful to point out, that (as was argued in the chapter in our first Part on the teaching of Augustine) the notion of creation, which the scriptural history, when its language is examined, presents to the thoughtful mind, is that the material creation with its living forms, is the development or evolution manifested in Time of that which before existed potentially in the Eternal Mind of the Creator; and was the seed from which the whole proceeded from age to age of the genesis. It is in no sense scientific, and without doubt it is utterly unphilosophical, to believe that life may proceed spontaneously—that is, without a cause—from that which is not living, but cannot proceed from the Ever-living and Almighty Spirit.

But the next question to be considered is, what explanation does science give of that which is an undoubted fact in creation, both as it exists at the present hour, and as it was in past ages, as we learn from the testimony of the rocks? In these we find fossil forms of the full-grown vegetation of former ages, while the genesis of the world that now is was proceeding. On the other hand, science now, in the present day, can trace, and has traced most carefully and completely, the development of the plant from its first beginning to its maturity. And we are here met by the remarkable and suggestive fact, that the very same conclusion to which science directed us, as to the formation of the inorganic part of the universe, is exactly applicable, *mutatis mutandis*, to the growth of each individual *living* organism, whether vegetable or animal.

That from which the organism is evolved is a homogeneous structureless germ, and the evolution is effected by the matter passing, both as regards its external form and its internal structure, from a state of indefinite, incoherent homogeneity, to one of definite coherent heterogeneity, through the agency of causes of which some and their laws are partially known to science, and others altogether unknown.

That the germ is structureless is assumed by modern physicists, and it certainly has no structure that the microscope can discover. Clerk Maxwell has proceeded further, and argued that it is impossible it should have, in consequence of the size of the smallest molecules; but this is questioned by some scientists, who imagine (it seems) a kind of mechanical structure which determines the future growth of the plant. However, this certainly is *not* evolution, but a modification of the old hypothesis of *emboîtement;* which supposed the whole future plant to be contained in miniature in the germ, as the language of Augustine shows was believed in his day. The present hypothesis of evolution is not only more philosophical, but much more scientific,—that is, much more in accordance with the facts observed in the growth both of the plant and of the embryo. And evolution (I would call special attention to this fact on the part of those who are frightened at the very name) when examined, is much less materialistic than any previous hypothesis; in fact, it is impossible to reconcile evolution with mere materialism; and it makes Augustine's illustration far more appropriate than he supposed it to be.

As regards that part of our definition of the development of the plant, which speaks of the *causes* of the evolution, no one will doubt that whatever may be known as to *some*,—such as the chemical action of the rays of the sun, the air, the dews of heaven, the soil in which it grows, and its other physical environments,—there is not a single herb of the field, however simple, the growth of which is not a profound mystery. Science may be able, to a limited extent, to explain, on principles known to itself, the causes of certain differentiations and integrations in the development both of the plant and the embryo; and may prove, that if these causes are wanting, or imperfect, or excessive, the development will not be the normal evolution. But of the cause of that which is infinitely the most important factor in the development, viz., its being a reproduction of the individual living organism, or organisms, from which the germ itself came; that the plant has leaves and flowers and seed of the same form and colour and fragrance,—except so far as they may be slightly modified by environments; that germs, "microscopic portions of seemingly structureless matter," should grow one into a fowl, another into a crocodile, and another into a dog;—to account for all this and much more besides, "we have," Herbert Spencer says, "to fall back upon *the unexplained principle of hereditary transmission;*" in fact, upon a "*mysterious property,*" of which science can merely observe the phenomena.

We find, therefore, that the causes of the growth of each individual plant and animal are—though we are so familiar with the phenomena of growth that they are taken as a matter of course, which nature does of itself—yet really as inconceivable by the human mind as is the creation of heaven and earth; and when it comes to be investigated, must be described, from the aspect of science, in almost the same language.

And may not this instructive analogy which science supplies help us and encourage us to proceed a step further, as to the development of the whole vegetable and animal kingdoms? We have seen, in the sixth chapter of this Part, in examining the "Law of Evolution," that in the animal kingdom at least, there was strong *prima facie* evidence for the development of the different species from the lowest to the highest, being somewhat similar to that of the growth of a living organism; so strong indeed, that it has naturally given a great impulse in modern times to the inquiry into the causes which may, to some extent, have produced these changes.

Every one knows the name of the late Charles Darwin as an author of a theory intended to explain how the evolution of the whole empire of organic life was effected; and everyone also knows how vehement has been the opposition which it has encountered, not merely from theologians, but, at first, from men of science also. And every one, unhappily, knows further, how by men who are ready to accept any theory without questioning, which they can turn into an argument against the belief in a Creator generally, and against Christianity in particular,—the theory of "evolution" by "natural selection" has been used far and wide to the prejudice of religion.

Professor St. George Mivart gives, in his work on the "Genesis of Species,"* the following brief statement of the Darwinian theory of *Natural Selection :*—

"Every kind of animal and plant tends to increase in numbers in a geometrical progression.

"Every kind of animal and plant transmits a general likeness, with individual differences, to its offspring.

"Every individual may present minute variations, of any kind and in any direction.

"Past time has been practically infinite.

"Every individual has to endure a very severe struggle for existence, owing to the tendency to geometrical increase of all kinds of animals and plants, while the total animal and vegetable population (man and his agency excepted) remains almost stationary.

* Pp. 9, 10.

"Thus every variation of a kind tending to save the life of the individual possessing it, or to enable it more surely to propagate its kind, will in the long run be preserved, and will transmit its favourable peculiarity to some of its offspring, which peculiarity will become intensified till it reaches the maximum degree of utility. On the other hand, individuals presenting unfavourable peculiarities will be ruthlessly destroyed. The action of this law of natural selection may thus be well represented by the convenient expression '*survival of the fittest.*'"

Sir John Lubbock, in enumerating, in his presidential address to the British Association in 1881, the discoveries and theories of the last fifty years, has of course referred to the promulgation of this theory by Darwin (and Wallace also independently) in the latter half of the previous half century. He gives as the four axioms on which the theory is based:

1. That no two animals or plants in nature are identical in all respects.

2. That the offspring tend to inherit the peculiarities of their parents.

3. That of those that come into existence, only a small number reach maturity.

4. That those which are, on the whole, best adapted to the circumstances in which they are placed, are most likely to leave descendants.

Sir John Lubbock adds, what is most important to be remembered, that Darwin, "while showing the great importance of natural selection," yet "attributed to it no exclusive influence, but fully admitted that other causes— the use and disuse of organs, sexual selection, etc.—had to be taken into consideration." He continues:—

"No one, at any rate, will question the immense impulse

which Darwin has given to the study of natural history, the number of new views he has opened up, and the additional interest which he has aroused in, and contributed to, Biology. When we were young we knew that the leopard had spots, the tiger was striped, and the lion tawny; but why this was so it did not occur to us to ask; and if we had asked no one would have answered. Now we see at a glance that the stripes of the tiger have reference to its life among jungle-grasses; the lion is sandy, like the desert; while the markings of the leopard resemble spots of sunshine glancing through the leaves. Again, Wallace in his charming essays on natural selection has shown how the same philosophy may be applied even to birds' nests—how, for instance, open nests have led to the dull colour of hen birds; the only British exception being the kingfisher, which, as we know, nests in river-banks. Lower still, among insects, Weismann has taught us that even the markings of caterpillars are full of interesting lessons; while, in other cases, specially among butterflies, Bates has made known to us the curious phenomena of mimicry."

But while it is impossible for any one, who is not either ignorant or prejudiced, to fail to acknowledge that the theory of natural selection which bears the name of Dr. Darwin has thrown a flood of light on the development of organic life, it is no less certain that there are apparently insuperable objections to this theory as accounting, except as one cause among others far more powerful, for the evolution of the vegetable and animal kingdom. Some of these objections have been urged with great force by Professor Mivart. These he sums up as follows* :—

That "natural selection" is incompetent to account for the incipient stages of useful structures.

* "Genesis of Species," p. 21. Darwin himself acknowledged the

That it does not harmonize with the co-existence of closely similar structures of diverse origin.

That there are grounds for thinking that specific differences may be developed suddenly instead of gradually.

That the opinion that species have definite though very different limits to their variability is still tenable.

That certain fossil transitional forms are absent which might have been expected to be present.

That some facts of geographical distribution supplement other difficulties.

That the objection drawn from the physiological difference between "species" and "races" still remains unrefuted.

That there are many remarkable phenomena in organic forms upon which "*natural selection*" throws no light whatever, but the explanations of which, if they could be attained, might throw light on specific origination.

It is quite possible that the progress of science may have modified some of these objections; it has also of late years produced from palæontology some confirmations, or supposed confirmations, of the theory. Lubbock says, in the Address from which I have already quoted, after referring to the importance of embryology as the key to the laws of animal development :—

"Thus the young of existing species resemble in many cases the mature forms which flourished in ancient times. Huxley has traced up the genealogy of the horse to the Miocene Anchitherium, and his views have since been remarkably confirmed by Marsh's discovery of the Pliohippus, Protohippus, Miohippus, and Mesohippus, leading down from the Eohippus of the early tertiary strata. In the same way Gaudry has called attention to the fact that

" admirable art and force " with which Mivart illustrated these objections to his theory as any complete explanation of the evolution of organic life.

just as the individual stag gradually acquires more and more complex antlers, having at first only a single prong, in the next year two points, in the following three, and so on; so the genus, as a whole, in Middle Miocene times, had two pronged horns; in the Upper Miocene, three; and that it is not till the Upper Pliocene that we find any species with the magnificent antlers of our modern deer. It seems to be now generally admitted that birds have come down to us through the Dinosaurians, and, as Huxley has shown, the profound break once supposed to exist between birds and reptiles has been bridged over by the discovery of reptilian birds and bird-like reptiles; so that, in fact, birds are modified reptiles. Again, the remarkable genus Peripatus, so well studied by Moseley, tends to connect the annulose and articulate types."

But illustrations of the theory, such as these, do not remove some of the objections raised by Mivart; much less do they in the least degree affect, except to confirm, other objections that are absolutely fatal to the theory of natural selection being ever accepted in philosophy or science as *the* cause of the evolution of animal and vegetable life. These are,—

First, that it is not a *true cause* at all; being merely a negative explanation. Nature selects those whose organization is suited for its requirements, through the failure of those that are not suited. But the theory supplies no explanation whatever of that which is necessary to make it complete, the *positive* tendency in animal and vegetable life to be evolved so as to be adapted for its environments. Without this, *natural selection* is nothing else than the old theory of chance, attributed to Democritus, which modern science has proved to have no foundation in the formation of the inorganic universe; and no one certainly, in any age, could have supposed natural selection to be the cause of the growth of a plant, or an animal, from its first germ to maturity. So that if we should suppose natural selection to be *the* cause of the evolution of the vegetable and animal kingdoms into their present condition, it would be without any parallel or analogy whatever, either in the inorganic or the organic universe.

This objection, in another form, has been very clearly put by one who certainly has no prejudice in favour of the Christian faith. Mr. Graham says,* in referring to Darwin's theory :—" In my own opinion, the difficulty the hypothesis labours under is simply the tremendous, and all but incredible, range of effects of which *natural selection* is the only explanation offered, and which, if its pretensions are to be justified, it must actually have accomplished. For we are asked to believe that natural selection evolved or made the thousands and tens of thousands of species of plants and animals from a 'few primordial forms.' . . . Besides the species, natural selection made the music of the bird, the beauty of the flower, the thought of the man ; for beyond natural selection, and the facts of adaptation and inheritance, no other causes are offered ;—and all these different effects, when we view them in their totality, are so prodigious in comparison with the cause assigned, that the hypothesis seems wholly incredible. That natural selection, the seizing hold of an *accidental variation* useful to the individual, according favour to its possessor in the struggle for existence, and transmitting the advantage to the next generation; that a constant repetition of this simple process should alone have accomplished all the marvels of organic creation, . . . seems too futile an explanation to be seriously believed or entertained."

* " Creed of Science," p. 33.

2. There is another objection, which, though not so fundamental from the side of philosophy, yet on the side of science is even more fatal to natural selection being accepted as the true cause of the evolution. I mean, that while natural selection may be sufficient to account for many *changes*,—say, for example, of the long neck of the giraffe, because it gives him an advantage in feeding on the lofty trees in Africa,—yet it does not follow *as a general rule* that the changes which aid in the struggle for existence are at all in the direction of *evolution*, that is, development. Sometimes, indeed, they may be in exactly the contrary direction. For instance, the case of the successive varieties of the horse to which Sir John Lubbock refers, and of which some so-called evolutionists have made so much, is apparently an example of *natural selection* and the "*survival of the fittest*," but it is *not* an example of evolution, but of the contrary; for the change has been from a well-developed hand of four fingers, through a process of inferior development from age to age, till the final result of *natural selection* is the horse of the present day, with its forefoot consisting of a single chain of four bones, one of which is enclosed in the hoof, a hugely exaggerated nail. The discovery of this series is adduced as of "supreme importance" in regard to the "doctrine of *evolution*." But it seems that some naturalists, in their interest in the theory of natural selection, forget that the only strictly scientific value that theory possesses is, so far as it can be proved to be a cause of *scientific development*, that is, evolution. Otherwise it must be a hindrance rather than an aid to the evolution of animal life; as in this case it certainly has been.

Combining together all these considerations, we cannot be far wrong in extending the same conclusion which we found applicable in its principles alike to the formation of the inorganic universe, and to the growth of each living organism to the whole organic universe; again of course *mutatis mutandis.*

The evolution of the organic material universe has been, both in the vegetable and in the animal kingdom, through gradual changes from individuals of comparatively indefinite incoherent homogeneity, to those of more and more definite and coherent heterogeneity, produced by the agency of causes of which some are partially known to science, and others altogether unknown.*

It need hardly be observed that this, referring only to the *material* universe, does not include man *as a rational and spiritual being;* of that question we shall treat briefly, so far as may be necessary for this treatise, in the next chapter.

But as regards the genesis of the material creation, the definition is scientifically complete. It does not profess to understand or to explain what is the positive cause that has given this tendency in the kingdoms of animated nature to progress in the direction of more fully developed forms; any more than we can explain or understand what is the true cause (under God) of the growth of a plant or an animal. We have only to compare the two cases of the evolution of the individual living organism and of the whole system, to perceive that, however different in the particulars, the underlying principle is identical. But if we are guided by this analogy in the general principle, there is one application of it which it is important to observe.

In regard to some of the objections to the sufficiency of the theory of natural selection to account for the "innate tendency" of certain groups of animal nature to develop peculiarities of a special kind, Professor Mivart remarks †

---

* See Note M, in Appendix.
† "Genesis of Species," p. 235.

that, "It is, to say the least, probable that other influences exist, terrestrial and cosmical, as yet unnoted," which might have special effects on some animal natures rather than others, and he continues:—

"If in the past history of the planet more causes ever intervened, or intervened more energetically than at present, we might *à priori* expect a richer and more various evolution of forms, more radically differing than any which could be produced under conditions of more perfect equilibrium. At the same time, if it be true that the last few thousand years have been a period of remarkable and exceptional uniformity as regards this planet's astronomical relations, there are then some grounds for thinking that organic evolution may have been exceptionally depressed during the same period."

The analogy which has guided us to the general principle of the development of the animal kingdom, strongly confirms, as I suggested in my article on Evolution in the *Church Quarterly*, this view of more causes intervening, or the same causes intervening more energetically, in the past history of the earth. The authors of "The Unseen Universe"* have referred to this as "an exceedingly valuable suggestion in comparing together the life history of the individual and that of the earth," so that I may be excused for giving the passage at length. "It must," it is observed, "be remembered that in the generation of the higher animal organisms, there are two stages of their evolution, which in the vertebrate animals are absolutely distinct—one from the germ to the birth, the time when the embryo becomes the animal; the other from the birth of the animal to its maturity. The former of these, though very much the

* "Paradoxical Philosophy: a Sequel to 'The Unseen Universe,'" p. 111 (*note*).

shorter period, is yet incomparably the most important, and that in which the characteristic features of the organism are developed. In the latter, the changes are confined to an enlargement of the form, the complete development of some parts of the structure and of the functions which arise from them, hardening of the bones, more distinct definition of the members, with some alterations in colour, texture, and other quite secondary and subordinate characters of the organism. All these have a very limited range, and bear no comparison at all with the growth from the germ to the perfected embryo; and yet, during this period exclusively, as a general rule, the variations caused by the external conditions and environments of the organism are produced. We may then (speaking generally) divide the evolution of higher animal life into two distinct periods—one very brief, during which infinitely the greater part of the development takes place, that development being determined chiefly by the 'law of hereditary transmission,' and only exceptionally by external conditions; the second, far more prolonged, during which the growth to maturity takes place, which is comparatively within very narrow limits, and is more or less modified by external circumstances. Now, if we are directed by the teaching of embryology to the analogy of a general evolution of the system of nature, the first question that presents itself seems to be this. If the evolution of the animal system is to be inferred from the evolution of the individual organism, must we not also suppose that there is in the former that which is analogous to their two distinct stages of evolution? In other words, must there not have been one period of what we might call the *genesis* of nature (corresponding to that of incubation), during which the chief part of the evolution took place; and a second, during which various limited changes have been produced, these being much affected by the varying conditions of the different parts of the system?

"It seems that the whole question resolves itself into the two following separate questions:—First, is there reason to believe that the animal kingdom (for to this part of the subject our inquiries must be confined) has been brought into its present state through a process of evolution of some kind or other? Secondly, is there ground for supposing that conditions or agencies now affecting animal organisms are sufficient to account for the whole evolution, or is the conclusion to which analogy points the more probable and rational, namely, that by far the greater part of the development was effected during a period of genesis, when processes were in operation, very different indeed from those of which we have now experience, processes of which we are just as incapable of forming any conception, as a man, who had only observed the growth of a chick into a full-grown fowl, would be of understanding how the chick itself is formed within the eggshell."

This hypothesis of a special evolution taking place during the period of creation, in the sense in which that word is used in Scripture,* completes the parallel that has been already traced between the scientific aspect of creation and that faith which Revelation teaches, so far as regards the *material* universe.

The importance of the hypothesis, in a scientific point of view, as accounting for the development of the vegetable and animal kingdom in a shorter period than would be possible if each new species were to be evolved merely by the repetition of infinitesimal variations, is considerable; for the time which astronomy and the physical laws of heat indicate as that during which life could have

* See Part I., chapter vii., p. 80.

Organic Nature.

existed on the earth is about a hundred million years, while for evolution by natural selection Haeckel contends that many thousands of millions must have been required. But, from our point of view, the hypothesis is far more important, as illustrating, by an analogy the force of which no one can question, the meaning of the Evolution of the organic kingdoms. For no one can deny that the *chief cause* of the evolution of the embryo from the ovum to its birth—one which, though external circumstances may slightly affect it, and co-operate with it, yet is alone the *vera causa*—is that mysterious power or principle (as Spencer himself calls it) which the germ contained. And in regard to the creation of the body of man through evolution, which embryology seems to make it impossible to question, it is no less important as showing that this may have taken place at first through some process utterly different from "natural selection," or anything of the kind; and yet, in some way of which we have no example whatever in the present state of nature, may have been as true evolution as that by which the embryo, which in many of its stages resembles that of other animals, grows into a child.

CHAPTER IX.

CREATION OF MAN.

AS the purpose of this treatise embraced the relation of the faith as regards creation to physical science only, and not to moral and mental philosophy, it was unnecessary to discuss in the first part the Christian faith in regard to the creation of man as a moral and spiritual being, made in the image and likeness of his Maker. This is a far more profound truth, and if the creation of the material universe is "unthinkable," that of man is an infinitely higher mystery; and yet it is that which, of all God's works in creation, speaks most directly to the spiritual intelligence of man himself. But the relation of this truth to other spheres of human knowledge would require a whole treatise at least as large as this to itself; and it is therefore only in those points in which the creation of man touches the sphere of physical science that it will be necessary to refer to it.

To enable us to discuss this question, it is sufficient to observe that Holy Scripture gives some very definite indications, as to the connexion which the creation of man holds to the creation of the rest of the animal kingdom. One is given in the fact that, in the inspired history of creation, the creation of man has not a day to itself; it is not *in this respect* separated from the creation of the

Creation of Man.

higher animals, so widely as this is from the creation of the vegetable kingdom. "Man is thus reminded that he has, in common with other animals, a material frame composed of the same constituents as theirs; that his body is but the perfection of animal organization: indeed, that in some respects the very beasts of the field are his superiors, if he does not realize his own true position as man."* This indication was long since noticed by the philosophical mind of St. Augustine, who observes,† "Hic animadvertenda quædam et conjunctio, et discretio animalium. Nam eodem die factum hominem dicit, quo bestias. Sunt enim omnia terrena animantia." The second indication is given in the second chapter of Genesis, where the creation of man is described more in detail, and is represented as a twofold act. "*The Lord God formed man of the dust of the ground, and breathed into his nostrils the breath of life, and man became a living soul.*" ‡ It must be noticed that the formation of the body of man is described in the same language as that of the animals. *Both were alike from the earth. But the gift of the living soul comes direct from God.* It is this of which Christ says, "*What shall a man give in exchange for his soul?*"

It is evident, therefore, that the Christian faith as to the creation of man, far from being disturbed, is confirmed and illustrated by any proofs that science may supply, as to the body of man being the result of processes somewhat similar to those by which the lower animal creation were

---

* *Pulpit Commentary.* "Introduction to the Pentateuch," p. vii.

† "De Genesi Lib. Imperf.," § 55.

‡ Gen. ii. 7. Cf. 1 Cor. xv. 45, from which it is evident that St. Paul understands the language not of animal life merely, but as including that rational life which man has by creation, as distinguished from animal life on the one hand, and from the spiritual life he receives from Christ on the other.

produced. It does not belong to physical science, but to other knowledge altogether, in fact most of all to religion itself, to show that man possesses another existence totally different from that which any animal possesses, and which, being of another character altogether, cannot be evolved out of an animal nature, but must be communicated directly from God Himself.

The truth of this twofold action in the creation of man is illustrated and confirmed by the process through which each individual man is brought into the world. No one will dispute the fact that man's body grows in the womb through a series of changes similar to that by which other animals are evolved. The Psalmist, we have seen,* refers to this process as an evidence of the Divine wisdom and goodness, and does not consider it inconsistent with the truth that God has made man but little lower than the angels. Solomon alludes to it † as one of those natural mysteries which human wisdom cannot fathom. But the soul which is akin to God is another matter altogether. Into the inquiry when or how the true personality of each man begins, we need not enter; the whole question is so far beyond the range of finite thought and "discourse of reason," that any attempt to understand it only involves us in irreconcilable contradiction. We know the spiritual being of man in which he is God's image, even as we know God Himself,—only by the manifestation of that mystery in human life.

But it may be asked, does physical science, though it cannot reveal the soul of man by the examination of his material form and structure, yet point to any outward and visible signs, which may aid faith, in an indirect and supplementary way, in regard to this part of God's

* Page 149 *supra*. † Eccles. x. 5.

Creation of Man. 197

creation? Undoubtedly there are such indications, sufficient to confirm the belief of those who are convinced (as surely every impartial mind must be) that man by his reason, by language, by his power of abstract thought, by his capacity for civilization and progress, and all those moral and spiritual faculties which are akin to the Divine, is in a totally different sphere from the brute creation. Yet it is probable that, to those who can see in man nothing more than an improved ape,—no, that appears to be unscientific; let us say an evolved zoophyte,—to kill whom (? which) is no murder, and to plunder whom is no theft, they may seem insufficient to mark so immense a gulf as we believe to exist between man and the mere animal. But this is due to the very fact, that the distinctive attributes of humanity are not merely superior to those of the animal in degree, but they transcend them altogether in kind; the superiority of mankind is spiritual, not material, and therefore is not such as can be expressed in material characters, or leave any broad and strongly marked signs in the animal nature of man. For instance, though the brain is certainly, of all organs in the body, that by which the intelligence is exercised, yet every fissure and fold in the brain of man has its analogy in the orang, the chimpanzee, and the gorilla. Huxley remarks that as regards the organization of the brain,—and surely by that, if by anything material, man's superiority should be indicated,—"the brain of man differs far less from that of the chimpanzee, than that of the latter does from the pig's brain."* So slight is the physical difference, in the very organ of intelligence, between him who weighs the stars, and makes the light tell its secrets as to the constitution of distant worlds; who by discovering and obeying the laws of nature makes it

* "Anatomy of Vertebrate Animals," p. 69.

serve his purposes; who lives and dies for sublime ideas; and above all, who is capable of believing and loving and serving the God of heaven and earth;—between such an one and the howling senseless brute who lives merely to satisfy his animal appetites. There can be no more convincing proof that the soul of man cannot be material. The very resemblance of man's physical nature to that of some members of the brute creation, proves beyond doubt that his superiority to them is *hyper-physical;* and therefore that it is impossible that his soul could have been derived from them by evolution. And thus physical science does indirectly, but very emphatically, confirm the faith which Revelation teaches, that man was created by God in His image.

We must expect, however, that any direct and positive evidences of this truth that physical science may supply, will be, so to speak, delicate and almost impalpable. They consist chiefly in indications that the body of man possesses from the first a physical organization suitable for the exercise of the distinctive faculties of humanity; in other words, that in man *capacity precedes culture.* For example, it seems certain that the power of human thought is ordinarily proportionate to the size of the brain. Men much distinguished for mental force have, as a general rule, unusually large brains. The average weight of the brain of man is forty-eight ounces: the brain of Cuvier weighed sixty-four ounces.* There is an appreciable difference in the average size of the brain among the more degraded races of mankind and that of the civilized races; and yet there are found, even among the lowest savages, many with brains equal to those of the average European. But, according to Virchow (in a remarkable passage in his Address quoted by me in the article on Evolution), and as

* Bain's "Mental Science," p. 5.

seems to be now generally admitted, the fossil skulls of the earliest human inhabitants of our globe are at least equal in their cranial cavity to those of men of the nineteenth century; which though it may not prove culture, at all events indicates capacity for the highest culture and civilization. Mr. Wallace—to whom the discovery of the effect of natural selection is due not less than to Darwin, though he questions, with reason, whether natural selection can account for the physical origin of man—has pointed out other proofs that the physical endowments of man are such as are far in excess of the use he makes of them in a savage state.* For example, the hand contains latent capacities and powers, which are unused by savages, and must have been even less required by palæolithic man and his still ruder predecessors. "It has all the appearance of an organ prepared for civilized man, and one which was required to make civilization possible." The same reasoning applies to the "wonderful power, range, and flexibility of the musical sounds producible by the human larynx;" and to the wonderful faculty, due to the extraordinary delicacy and refinement of the internal organization of the ear, of appreciating musical tones and the harmony of chords.

That man therefore, who, as is indicated both in Holy Scripture and by science, was on the one side of his being produced as other living organisms were, and, as each individual man is himself at the present day, through a process of evolution, was nevertheless in his complete being a Divine work of a totally different order from evolution, even physical science itself not obscurely suggests. What that work was, beyond being a manifestation in time of the idea in the Eternal and Infinite Mind of God, Father, Son, and Holy Ghost, it would be altogether out of place to

* See "Genesis of Species," p. 278.

speculate. The notion "that, at a certain epoch in the world's history, mental and moral powers were conferred by Divine interposition on some animal that had been gradually modified in its bodily structure by natural causes till it took the form of man," is not only, as Professor Stokes says, "somewhat grotesque," but altogether unphilosophical, and inadmissible. It is as though we should argue that the embryo suddenly becomes a rational and spiritual being when it has all its physical development. But are we not in error in introducing the condition of *time* at all into the question? Man's soul belongs to eternity, his body only to time.

I ought, in concluding this portion of the treatise (chapters vii., viii., ix.), in which much use is made of the argument of analogy, to remind my readers of the precedents for such use in the teaching even of our Lord Himself, and, at more length, in that of the Apostle Paul. The parables of Christ may indeed be considered as illustrations, rather than arguments; but there is one instance, in which He so emphasizes an illustration from God's operations in nature, that it must be regarded as an argument. "Verily, verily, I say unto you" (were His words shortly before His own death), "Except a grain of wheat fall into the earth and die, it abideth by itself alone; but if it die, it bringeth forth much fruit" (John xii. 24). St. Paul uses the same analogy in the fifteenth chapter of the First Epistle to the Corinthians; and (in the twelfth chapter of the same Epistle) the analogy of the human body, as supplying arguments as to the Church of Christ, and in both cases very expressly and fully. From the religious or theological side, therefore, there ought to be no objection to arguments from analogy. And certainly if the analogy of the natural world may direct us in matters of religion, much more must it be a legitimate guide in regard to the physical world itself.

CHAPTER X.

LAW OF DECAY.

IN works on the evidences of religion, no argument derived from the scientific aspects of creation has so much prominence as the "teleological," the argument from design. The evidences in support of this argument are abundant in every department of science.* And the argument is not only used largely and with much force by Christian writers of all ages, and is implied in Scripture itself, but is employed by heathen writers of antiquity. Some modern scientists now urge that the theory of "natural selection" and the "law of evolution" sufficiently account for all that used to be attributed to design; because if we find organic forms adapted to their environments, we need not attribute this to design, since it would as surely be the effect of "natural selection" and the "struggle for existence," which would permit no form to be perpetuated which is not so adapted. But, on the one hand, as has been before observed, "natural selection" is only a negative explanation, and no positive cause at all of the adaptation. Besides which, the hypothesis of mutual adaptation can only account for the evidences in favour of design from one

---

* I know no work in which they are accumulated with more learning and skill, than in the Appendix (Notes xii. to xxi. inclusive) to Professor Flint's "Theism," the Baird Lecture for 1876.

particular sphere of creation, and does not touch the general argument, from the harmony of the inorganic world with the vegetable, the animal, and the human existences; and of these one with another.* Indeed, the well-known design argument of Paley from the watch,—an argument which was anticipated by Cicero in his work *De Natura Decorum*, where he supposes an orrery which had been invented in his day, and imitated the motions of the heavenly bodies, to be carried to a barbarous country,†—has only received increased force from the very theory that is supposed to overthrow it. Huxley's answer to Paley is one, the *reductio ad absurdum* of which one can only wonder that so acute a mind did not perceive. It is this: that if we suppose that it could be shown that the perfect watch was the result of a series of modifications of something originally quite rudimentary, and "that all these changes had resulted, first, from a tendency in the structure to vary indefinitely, and secondly, from something in the surrounding world which helped all variation in the direction of an accurate timekeeper, and checked all those in the other direction, then the force of Paley's argument would be gone." One would have supposed, that if the man who found the watch discovered further that it was the result of other self-adjusting machinery, through which all the parts of the watch were gradually formed in the proper shape, so it became at last an accurate timekeeper, his conviction that it was the result of design would be a hundredfold increased!

We have, however, approached the subject of the relation of science to faith from a different side altogether from that of the evidences of Christianity. Our purpose is to show that since faith teaches that creation is the result of the

* Address to Victoria Institute, p. 11.
† Referred to in Appendix to Flint's "Theism."

Law of Decay.

wisdom of God, science, so far as it explains nature to us truly, cannot fail to aid faith by expounding the result of that wisdom. Of course since wisdom includes,* as we have seen, "striving after the best ends as well as using the best means," it necessarily involves the idea of design. But there is a logical flaw in the argument from design,—unless we mean by it merely a contrivance for a subordinate end,—to which I think sufficient attention has not been paid. Design includes no doubt the idea of the use of means for a certain end; but besides the question, which are the *best* means, there is the far more important one which creation raises, what are the ends which infinite and unsearchable wisdom contemplates therein? It might have been and has been supposed that the creation of God must have been a universe without any defects, without any wastes, without any noxious herbs and destructive animals, with no tendency to change, no suffering, and above all with no death. The fact that the condition of nature is, in all these respects, different from that which might have been expected from an almighty and beneficent Creator, has in all ages been urged against the argument from design as a proof of the existence of such a Creator. Nor has the only complete reply to that objection always been given with sufficient distinctness,—I mean that Infinite Wisdom may have ends and purposes in creation, of which we know nothing at all at present; and that it has already revealed to us some ends, which are at least sufficient to account for the anomalies to which these objectors point.

The fact of the creation of God being subject to "vanity," or to "a law of decay," which has been discussed in the first part of this treatise, is itself one of those apparent anomalies. This Revelation affirms to have been the result

* See Part I., chap. iv., p. 49.

of the will of an all-wise God, and it directs us, not obscurely, to the end and purpose of this anomaly. That creation is subject to this law is a truth, of which science has given in modern times some unexpected and very remarkable confirmations.

Of course the fact that nature, as it exists in the present constitution of the world, including man himself, is under this law of decay, is obvious enough without the teaching of science. But modern theology, with hardly an exception, used to teach that this condition of nature was entirely due to the entrance of sin into the world through man's fall, and that, to use the words of a popular divine of the beginning of this century,* "This world was originally formed to be a delightful residence. Its surface was beautiful, its soil fertile without decay, its seasons vernal, its atmosphere, waters, and productions pregnant with life; and all its inhabitants" (the imaginative writer seems to suppose the state of man's innocence to have been a considerable period) "pacific, useful, and happy. In the country of Eden 'the Lord God also planted a garden, to become the appropriate residence of the first man; and here He made to grow every tree that is pleasant to the sight and good for food. This paradise was the beautiful metropolis of a beautiful world." It is not to be supposed, the preacher elsewhere says, that "the world came from the hands of God that mass of inclemency, barrenness, and confusion which we see in its present state." And of course the necessary conclusion from this was that the animals themselves were not subject to suffering and death. Even to the present day, indeed, some—happily very few—theologians persist in believing that no animals died before the fall of man! How animals obtained the supernatural gift of immortality, and how the

* Dr. Dwight, Sermon xxiii.

earth was to have supported animal life, if the different species should increase and multiply, and death were not to thin their ranks, they do not explain. It needed not the teaching of science to convince the philosophic mind of Augustine that an animal body must be a mortal body. His argument that our body is *dead*, and not merely *mortal*, on account of sin,—for it was from the first mortal through the necessary condition of an animal body,*—shows that he assumed that animals were subject to death.

Yet there is no doubt that it was a rude shock to the modern religious mind, when geology revealed the truth that the animal creation was subject to death from its very commencement, for ages before man appeared on the earth. And this truth was emphasized by the discovery, that not only was there death from the beginning, but there were, before the fall, destructive animals on the earth; as was proved by the fossil remains of some caught, by some violence of nature or otherwise, *in flagrante delicto*, in the very act of destruction with their prey in their mouths. So that Buckland, in his Bridgewater Treatise on Geology, thought it necessary to apologize, as it were, for the existence of such animals in creation, on the ground (undoubtedly very true) that since animals were to die, it was a merciful provision, on the whole, that the surplus animal population should be carried off by their carnivorous brethren, instead of being left to perish miserably by slow decay.

However, although this truth became at last generally recognized, yet the theological mind does not seem to have fully realized that which analogy might have suggested, even if the teaching of St. Paul and other parts of Holy Scripture had not assured it, that this law of decay

* See Appendix, Note N.

to which all organic nature is subject, is that of the whole universe. When Laplace proved by mathematics that "the planetary system was stable, so that no one of the perturbations which planet produces upon planet can become so great as to cause a disruption or a permanent alteration in the planetary orbits; but that the law of gravitation secures that all such disturbances shall be periodic, so that after the lapse of millions of years the planets will all return to the same relative positions, and a new cycle of disturbances will commence," the discovery was regarded with satisfaction on the theological side. It certainly did not confirm the teaching of Scripture * that "the heavens should wax old as a garment, and as a mantle shalt Thou roll them up, and they shall be changed;" which in itself does sufficiently point to the whole created universe being subject to decay; but neither from this passage, nor from the teaching of St. Paul, was such a conclusion drawn, and Laplace's discovery was considered an additional proof of the wisdom of God in creation.

But, gradually, this discovery, though true as the solution of an abstract mathematical problem, on the supposition of there being no resisting medium, and no other bodies in the universe besides those of the solar system, and no unknown causes of change and decay in the system of the universe, was found to be untrustworthy as a proof of the eternal permanence of creation. First of all, the fact of the period of Encke's comet having gradually decreased from the first time of its observation between 1786 and 1789, led to the suspicion of a resisting medium, sufficient to retard the motion of such a body as a comet, and diminish its orbit; and though the existence of such

* Psalm cii. 26; Heb. i. 11, 12.

a medium is not (it seems) confirmed by other phenomena than those of the motions of comets, it yet called attention to the possible instability of the system of the universe. Then it was determined that there were causes *—one, the friction of the tides on the earth; the other, periods of manifestation of increased electrical intensity—which must result in loss of energy. Then the radiation of heat from all sources of heat like the sun,—which would have to be supplied, if supplied at all, by solid masses falling into it from time to time, or in some other way,—looked as if the universe were not eternal. And lastly the law of the "degradation of energy" was established by Sir William Thomson, the result of which must necessarily be that although the actual quantity of energy in the universe remain the same, the amount of *available* energy must always be steadily decreasing, so that it is as absolutely certain that the whole visible universe shall in its own time die, as it is that each vegetable and animal organism has its appointed time.†

The scientific reasoning on which this theory of the degradation of energy depends is far too abstruse to be intelligible to any but those who have carefully studied the laws of heat, as expounded by the most advanced physical science of modern times. A brief explanation of

* Jevons, ii., p. 44.
† The conclusion, at which Sir W. Thomson and the leading English mathematicians have arrived, is called in question by some German physicists, simply (it seems) on the ground of its being too like a discovery made in the interest of Christianity. But the fact in itself that bodies are observed in the heavens, in all stages of cosmical life, from that of Sirius (for example) to that of our moon, which is cosmically dead, is sufficient evidence that there is nothing in the system of the universe to supply the available energy which is lost by the heat constantly radiating into space.

it, however, is given in "The Unseen Universe,"* and even those who are unable to follow the arguments cannot fail (from a religious point of view) to be interested in the very singular conclusion at which Clerk Maxwell arrived, that the result as to the loss of available energy would be materially altered by the interposition of the action of finite intelligences, even without any addition of energy.

In fact, science confirms the conclusion to which the analogy of the organic creation would direct us, and which Revelation teaches, that the whole creation is made subject by God to "vanity" or instability, and the "law of decay."

* Articles 106—113 inclusive.

CHAPTER XI.

CONCLUSION.

1. IT must, I think, be sufficiently obvious to every one who takes the trouble to read carefully the arguments in this treatise from first to last, that a work which should attempt to answer the question proposed, as to the aid rendered by science to faith, merely by examining and discussing the conclusions, or accepted theories, of the science existing at the time when it was written, could be of very little permanent value. Indeed, if the views are correct which are expounded in the second chapter of the first part of this treatise, and confirmed (in the Note on that chapter) by the opinion of the late Clerk Maxwell, we must conclude that whatever temporary advantage might appear to be gained by the ingenious use of arguments suggested by modern scientific hypotheses or developments, the permanent result might be injurious, both to religion and to science. And therefore, in the second part of this treatise, while I have not hesitated to call attention occasionally to those results of modern science which seem to my own mind calculated to strengthen faith in God's Word; I have been anxious to direct the thoughts of my readers rather to general principles, which may include very different particular solutions of the problems of the universe, than to any such solutions themselves, however plausible.

There is much force in other words of the profound Christian philosopher to whom I have just referred, when he says that while he considers that "Christians whose minds are scientific are bound to study science, that their view of the glory of God may be as extensive as their being is capable of," yet (he adds), "I think that the results which each man arrives at, in his attempts to harmonize his science with his Christianity, ought not to be regarded as having any significance except to the man himself, *and to him only for a time.*"* And to the same effect elsewhere, while objecting to any attempt to interpret Scripture by scientific theories, he says, "At the same time, I think that each individual man should do all he can to impress his own mind with the extent, the order, and the unity of the universe, and should carry these ideas with him as he reads such passages as Colos. i., just as enlarged conceptions of the extent and unity of the world of life may be of service to us in reading Psalm viii., Heb. ii. 6, etc."† And this, in fact, as stated in the Introduction, is the purpose of this treatise; to suggest such lines of thought to individual believers as may confirm and strengthen and inform the faith of each. But I confess I look to its producing such a result, much more by directing their minds to the true import of the Christian faith as to creation, than by any direct confirmation of the faith from scientific theories or discoveries. In truth, so far as these are concerned (with the exception, perhaps, of the evidences of the subjection of the creation to the Law of Decay), the most satisfactory confirmation of the Christian faith, that science supplies in regard to creation, seems to me to be found in those things which many consider as contrary to faith in a Creator; I mean, the discoveries, so far as they are

* "Life," p. 405.   † *Ibid*, p. 394.

discoveries, that much in nature that used to be regarded as effected immediately by Divine Power, are the result of natural causes; for I am thus enabled to recognize more distinctly the presence of the Creator's wisdom everywhere throughout nature, even where before it was least apparent. And if we fully realize this, it will make us less reluctant to allow, even to those which appear somewhat crude and hasty scientific speculations, at least whatever value they may have as provisional hypotheses. I own there seems to me some force—though not so much as they claim—in the argument of a certain class of scientific men (those whom I have called "phenomenologists" as distinguished from the mathematicians and students of dynamical science), that while Christians claim belief in religious truths, though they admit such truths are not capable of exact logical proof, they yet refuse to give any credence to scientific theories, unless they are as certainly proved as a proposition in Euclid. The answer to this is of course obvious, that scientific truth is simply founded on the reason, or deduced by it; while with the belief of religious truth the conscience and the faculty of discerning spiritual good and evil are concerned. Yet it is also certain that in some departments of science there is an intuitive insight into the harmonies and laws of nature, which in some minds anticipates, if it does not supersede, the ordinary processes of reasoning; and by the aid of such insight some of the greatest discoveries of science have been made. And if we only understand the true vocation of science, we need not be jealous of the legitimate use of any of its functions, or of any of its inquiries as to the physical causes through which the wisdom of God has made nature such as it is. I cannot but believe that it would be an immense gain, both to theology and to science, if there were this feeling on both sides, that their true and, so to speak, natural relation to one another is that of friends and allies. It is evident that the first steps towards a reconciliation of this kind must be taken on the theological side, because theologians ought to be able to perceive more distinctly, and expound more fully, what the true relation between them is. It undoubtedly would be a great gain to us, on the side of the Christian faith, if in our conflict against the various forms of infidelity we could boldly and consistently take the ground, that far from being afraid of science and its discoveries, we consider all its discoveries as helping us to understand what God's work in creation means. Is it not the case, that at least half the popular prejudices against the Christian faith among the uneducated or half-educated classes, —must we not say also, among some of the most highly educated—which take the form of quasi-scientific objections, are due to theologians themselves, and to their avowed jealousy of some departments of science? And thus the idea becomes fixed in the popular mind, that Christianity is afraid of science because it cannot hold its own against it, and because our beliefs will not bear its light? While the better informed think, at all events, that there must be something in Christianity, at least in its orthodox form, which indisposes the mind, especially the clerical mind, to accept scientific truth. It surely would be no small gain to have the ground cleared of all such misapprehensions. And not only this, but to the believer himself it would be a great advantage to be wholly free from such apprehensions. It is surely our duty to believe firmly that the Creator has, as St. Paul teaches, given sufficient witness to Himself in His own works to leave men without excuse if they stifle and suppress that knowledge. And therefore if the interpretations of nature which some give do appear to us somewhat wide of the mark, and rather to obscure that witness, we need not be anxious, or attempt to confirm God's own testimony by counter speculations of our own, perhaps even more crude and ill-founded. The injury of such attempts to defend Holy Scripture, or at least our own interpretations of it, is well described by the great St. Augustine in a passage quoted in our discussion of his teaching.* We may be content to await the progress of science, in which especially, as Bacon says, *Truth is the daughter of Time.*

II. It must, however, be observed, that while I speak of science as the natural and necessary ally of faith, and to be acknowledged and reverenced as such by all true Christians, I do not include in science speculations, whether modern or those of ancient Greek philosophy, which attribute the works of God in nature to some "*innate properties*" in matter itself. This is, in fact, not science at all, in any true sense of the word. It is not merely "unscientific," but quite as subversive of science as if theists should maintain that the present form and phenomena of nature are due to the immediate power of God without any intermediate physical causes. For science demands in nature a physical cause for a physical effect, and rejects "innate properties" as a metaphysical superstition which can only arrest the progress of true science; for *innate properties* mean effects without a cause.

Perhaps, however, it might be more correct to say that a question of this nature lies altogether beyond the sphere and range of physical science, and belongs to that of metaphysical philosophy; which indeed is not only the ultimate foundation of physical science itself, but will probably be, before long, the field on which the real con-

* Page 71.

flict between faith and unbelief will have to be fought.* Hitherto the leaders of physical science in England have, with few exceptions, not only neglected but despised this philosophy, as one in which no certainty can be attained. But besides the instance to which I have before referred, of a scientific mind feeling the need of a higher philosophy than that of physical science to deal with the problem of the creation of the universe, it is very interesting to find Clerk Maxwell, in an address to the British Association on the relation of mathematics and physics, indicating, in a manner half humorous but very characteristic of himself, his sense of the need of metaphysical philosophy to explain even that relation. Having spoken of the different aspects of physical investigations and pure mathematics, he adds, "But who will lead me into that still more hidden and dimmer region, where thought weds fact,—where the mental operation of the mathematician and the physical action of the molecules are seen in their true relation? *Does not the way to it pass through the very den of the metaphysician, strewed with the remains of former explorers and abhorred by every man of science?*"

For reasons I have given already,† it is no part of my duty in this treatise to attempt to pass through that den.

III. But it may be said with truth, that there is one part of the Christian faith in regard to creation, of which no notice whatever has been taken in this treatise, though it is very distinctly revealed in Holy Scripture. I mean, that besides the creation of the visible universe, of which the first and second chapters of Genesis speak, there is an

* See pp. 112-114. I expressed the same opinion in a paper read at the Leeds Church Congress in 1871, on "Vital Christianity as affected by the Present State of Science and Civilisation."

† *Supra*, p. 113.

"unseen universe" which we also believe to have been created by God through His Eternal Word. This part of the Christian faith, which is explicitly asserted in the Nicene Creed, is expressly taught by St. Paul, who reminds us[*] that in Christ "were all things created, in the heavens and upon the earth, things visible and things invisible, whether thrones, or dominions, or principalities, or powers; all things have been created through Him and unto Him." That there is such an unseen universe, and that it is the creation of God no less than that which is material and visible, is implied throughout the whole of the Scriptures, both of the Old and of the New Testament.

Some ten years ago, nothing probably was further from the thoughts of those who took a general interest in the subject of the relations between science and religion, than that physical science, which had to deal with the problems of the visible universe, with that creation of God which is "seen and temporal," could in any degree aid us in realizing that which is "unseen and eternal." A philosophical man of science, perhaps, such as "the deservedly famous Dr. Thomas Young," could perceive that science did to a certain extent suggest the possibility, and indeed probability, of an unseen spiritual world even in the midst of us. But such ideas did not spread far even among educated minds; and there is no doubt that the general idea was, as Sir William Hamilton maintained, that if physicists speculated at all, it would be certainly in the direction of materialism. And by the Sadducæan school in this country and in Germany, who believe in nothing but the visible universe, it was supposed that in the present age, enlightened as it is by the discoveries of physical science, the very mention of angels and the unseen world in the Bible is quite sufficient

[*] Colos. i. 16.

of itself to disprove its truth as a history. But in 1875 the now famous work, "The Unseen Universe," appeared, at first published anonymously, but in the following year owned by the two great leaders of physical science, Professor Balfour Stewart and Professor Tait; and the authors of this work claimed, from a purely physical point of view, to prove the possibility, and indeed the antecedent probability, of an unseen universe which is not temporal, as the visible and grossly material universe must be, but eternal. To illustrate the possibility of this from physical considerations, they adopt the last scientific hypothesis of the atomic constitution of the visible universe as pointing to a possible constitution of the unseen universe, but they are careful to remind us that they do this for the sake of bringing their ideas in a concrete form before their readers, and "for this purpose" only. Their general reasoning would be equally applicable, if further investigations were to modify or even supersede the particular hypothesis as to the molecular constitution of the present universe.

Profoundly interesting as this work is, the subject could not have been discussed within the limits of the present treatise, which deals with difficulties relating to the creation of those things which are seen and temporal, which are the difficulties that more immediately affect ordinary Christians. For those who desire to know whether "science aids faith in regard to the creation of those things that are unseen," this reply, given by men whose scientific attainments and powers are acknowledged by all, is for the present quite sufficient. Perhaps when the physical theories discussed in "The Unseen Universe" have stood the test of some ten or fifteen years, there may be some one competent, from the theological side, to give another reply, yet more complete and convincing.

APPENDIX.

Note A. *Part I., chap. i., p. 18.*

On Gen. i. 22, which concluded in Augustine's version of the Scriptures with the words "*And it was so*," Augustine remarks ("De Genesi Imp.," Lib. 52), "Hic plane quivis tardus jam evigilare debet, ut intelligat quales isti dies enumerentur. Cum enim certos seminum numeros Deus animantibus dederit, servantes miram certo ordine constantiam, ut certo dierum numero, pro suo quoque genere, et concepta utero gerant, et edita ova calefaciant; . . . *quomodo uno die potuerunt et concipere et utero gravescere et parta nutrire et implere aquas maris et multiplicari super terram?*"

Note B. *Part I., chap. ii., p. 32.*

After this chapter was written, and in type, I saw for the first time, in the "Life of Professor Clerk Maxwell,"—certainly one of the most interesting and instructive biographies of the present day, both to the Christian and to the lover of science,—a letter from him to the Bishop of Gloucester and Bristol, which confirms so expressly and emphatically the objections I have urged against the attempt to interpret the scriptural history of creation by scientific theories, that I am thankful to confirm my argument by the independent opinions of such a man. I am the more anxious to do so, because to not a few reverent students of Holy Scripture the argument of this chapter will probably be far from acceptable, and may appear to be throwing away an advantage that modern science has providentially given to the Christian faith. The Bishop had written to Clerk Maxwell to ask his opinion, as a scientific man, as to the statement, on the theological side, that the creation of the sun posterior to light involves no serious difficulty, according to the views of modern science.

Clerk Maxwell's reply to this question is very instructive. He says,* "With respect to your second question, there is a statement printed in most commentaries that the fact of light being created before the sun is in striking agreement with the last results of science (I quote from memory). I have often wished to ascertain the date of the original appearance of this statement, as this would be the only way of finding what 'last results of science' it referred to. It is certainly older than the time when any notions of the undulatory theory became prevalent among men of science or commentators. *If it were necessary to provide an interpretation of the text in accordance with the science of* 1876 *(which may not agree with that of* 1896), *it would be very tempting to say* that the light of the first day means the all-embracing æther, the vehicle of radiation, and not actual light, whether from the sun or from any other source. But I cannot suppose that this was the very idea meant to be conveyed by the original author of the book to those for whom he was writing. He tells us of a previous darkness. Both light and darkness imply a being who can see if there is light, but not if it is dark, and the words are always understood so. That light and darkness are terms relative to the creature only is recognised in Psalm cxxxix. 12. As a mere matter of conjectural cosmogony, however, we naturally suppose those things most primeval which we find least subject to change. Now the æther or material substance which fills all the interspace between world and world, without a gap or flaw of $\frac{1}{100000}$ inch anywhere, and which probably penetrates through all grosser matters, is the largest, most uniform, and apparently most permanent object we know, and we are therefore inclined to suppose that it existed before the formation of the systems of gross matter which now exist within it, just as we suppose the sea older than the individual

---

* The italics are mine, and are intended to indicate the coincidence of the writer's views with those of this treatise.

fishes in it. *But I should be very sorry if an interpretation founded on a most conjectural scientific hypothesis were to get fastened to the text in Genesis*, even if by so doing it got rid of the old statement of the commentators which has long ceased to be intelligible. *The rate of change of scientific hypotheses is naturally much more rapid than that of biblical interpretations*, so that if an interpretation is founded on such an hypothesis, it may help to keep the hypothesis above ground *long after it ought to be buried and forgotten.*" (" Life of James Clerk Maxwell," pp. 393-394.)

It is impossible to refer to Clerk Maxwell without expressing one's thankfulness to Almighty God that, in these days, when so many imagine that Christianity is in danger from the progress of science, one was raised up,—to us it seems lost too soon,—who, while he opened to students of science almost a new world of knowledge, yet found science nothing but an aid to his simple and earnest faith in that Saviour on whom in life and in death he trusted.

NOTE C. *Part I., chap. iii., p.* 39.

It is certain that many animals, even some insects, not only distinguish colours, but also prefer some colours to others. As regards insects, it seems highly probable that for some physical reason, perhaps the chemical action of the different rays, one colour is more attractive and pleasant than another. It is difficult to conceive that bees, for example, prefer blue flowers to others, *cæteris paribus*,—as Sir J. Lubbock affirms, in a paper read at the meeting of the British Association in 1881,—except for some cause of this kind, which produces a pleasurable sensation in the organism, totally different from any sense of beauty. It may be from some such cause that on the other hand bulls are excited by a red object. Darwin, again, mentions, on Sir S. Baker's authority, that the African elephant and rhinoceros attack grey and white horses with special fury. A son of mine was once pursued by a rhinoceros because he had a white helmet on his head, and the chase ceased as soon as he concealed it. If indeed we are to believe Darwin in his work on Sexual Selection, animals must have some sense of beauty as regards colour. But the sole independent argument for this seems to be that as "we behold male birds elaborately displaying their plumes and splendid colours before the females, whilst other birds not thus decorated make no such display, it is impossible to doubt that the females admire the beauty of their male partners" (vol. i., pp. 63, 322). As the plain turkey-cock and the dowdy pigeon has action of somewhat the same kind when courting, it seems rather a large inference from uncertain premises. Of course the theory of the bright colours of some birds being due to sexual selection requires the hypothesis of their having some sense of beauty as regards colour. But Darwin himself allows that many animal organisms of the lowest classes, to which the theory of sexual selection cannot possibly apply, are ornamented with the most brilliant and gorgeous colours. And certainly the beauty of the colours of flowers, which are less brilliant than the tints with which animals are decorated, simply from the difference between vegetable and animal substance, sufficiently proves that God clothes His creatures with the beauty and variety of colour through some other causes than sexual selection, *if by that at all*. However the enjoyment of colour *in itself* seems, even in man, to be different from the higher perception of the beautiful.

NOTE D. *Part I., chap. iv., p.* 55.

Of all the attempts made by Jewish Rabbis or Christian theologians to improve on the simple meaning of God's Word by an allegorical or, as it is untruly called, a "spiritual sense,"— when the allegory does not arise out of the spiritual truth in the history itself,—few have been, as it seems to me, more irrelevant to the teaching of Holy Scripture than the interpretation of "Behemoth" and "Leviathan,"—which in this majestic description of God's creation are adduced as visible instances and notable proofs, in the world of nature, of the physical impotence and insignificance of man compared with God's works—as types and representatives of powers of spiritual wickedness. The whole force of the argument which is derived from the manifestation of the wisdom, goodness, and power of God in creation, and points us from these creatures of God to Him Who is the Maker of them all, as in the words I have quoted, is not merely obscured by such an allegory, but utterly destroyed. I observe that an eminent and profoundly learned commentator of the present day considers that every "reverent reader" of this book must be conscious that there is "an inconceivable *bathos*" here, unless we look for some allegorical meaning. But may we not recognize the sublimity and grandeur of the very simplest truth, when it is spiritual truth indeed? Must we—in order to discern the sublimity of our Lord's teaching, that not one of these sparrows, two of which are sold for a farthing, falls to the ground without our Father—look for an allegorical meaning and expound the sparrows here as types of the evil spirits which carry away the seed sown in our hearts? Yet such an exposition would hardly be more out of place and irrelevant to the true meaning of the text, than the allegorical interpretation of this passage in Job. A brief discussion of this question of allegory is contained in a following note.

NOTE E. *Part I., chap. vi., p.* 67.

Having referred to the difficulties which sincere Christians find in the beginning of Genesis, as contrasted with those which the Manichæans raised, he continues, " Sane quisquis voluerit omnia quæ dicta sunt secundum litteram accipere, id est non aliter intelligere quam littera sonat, et potuerit evitare blasphemias, et omnia congruentia fidei catholicæ prædicare, non solum ei non est invidendum, sed præcipuus multumque laudabilis intellector habendus est. Si autem nullus exitus datur ut pie et digne Deo quæ scripta sunt intelligantur, nisi figurate atque in ænigmatibus proposita ista credamus; habentes auctoritatem apostolicam, a quibus tam multa de libris Veteris Testamenti solvuntur ænigmata, modum quem intendimus teneamus, adjuvante illo qui nos petere quærere et pulsare adhortatur; ut omnes istas figuras rerum secundum catholicam fidem . . . explicemus, non praejudicantes meliori diligentiorique tractatui, sive per nos, sive per alios quibus Dominus revelare dignetur.

NOTE F. *Part I., chap. vi., p.* 68.

That the history of the creation of the material and natural world was even more than a mere allegory of the new creation, we may well admit. God's work, whether in the visible universe, or in that which is unseen, cannot but be the same fundamentally, since God is one. And therefore nature is full of parables. But it is well to remember *why* the Old Testament history, to which not only St. Paul but our Lord Himself refers as full of types and figures of the Gospel, is capable of an allegorical interpretation. It is, as is evident when we look beyond the letter to the spirit, because the history is that of God's dealings with man, and involves therefore the same principles fundamentally as those of the gospel. The history of the Old Testament is a figure of the New, being cast (as it were) in the same spiritual mould. The arbitrary and artificial resemblances, such as those of names and external circumstances, are entirely subordinate to the inner principles, and merely serve as hints to direct us to these. Compare, for example, the allegorical interpretation by St. Paul in Gal. iv. 21—31, with our Lord's reference to Moses raising up the serpent of brass, and (as an example among the numerous histories in Scripture which Christian thought cannot fail to recognize as typical of Christ) the history of Joseph. But it must be noticed that the value and force of the allegorical meaning depend on the literal reality of the history itself.

NOTE G. *Part I., chap. vi., p.* 68.

De Genesi contra Manich. Lib. i. (vii.) "Dictum est, *In principio fecit Deus cœlum et terram;* non quia jam hoc erat, sed quia hoc esse poterat: nam et cœlum scribitur postea factum. Quemadmodum si semen arboris considerantes, dicamus ibi esse radices, et robur, et ramos, et fructus, et folia; non quia jam sunt, sed quia inde futura sunt; sic dictum est, *In principio, etc.*, quasi semen cœli et terræ, cum in confuso adhuc esset cœli et terræ materies, sed quia certum erat inde futurum esse cœlum et terram, jam et ipsa materies cœlum et terra appellata est."

His more matured thoughts on the subject, to which I refer subsequently, he expresses thus in his "De Genesi ad Literam," Lib. v. (xxiii.) :—

"Consideremus ergo cujuslibet arboris pulchritudinem in robore, ramis, frondibus, pomis : hæc species non utique repente tanta ac talis est exorta, sed quo etiam ordine novimus. Surrexit enim a radice, quam terræ primum germen infixit; atque inde omnia illa formata et distincta creverunt. Porro illud germen ex semine ; in semine ergo illa omnia fuerunt primitus, non mole corporeæ magnitudinis, sed vi potentiaque causali. . . .

"Sicut autem in ipso grano invisibiliter erant omnia simul quæ per tempora in arborem surgerent ; ita ipse mundus cogitandus est, cum Deus simul omnia creavit, habuisse simul omnia, quæ in illo et cum illo facta sunt, quando factus est dies ; non solum cœlum cum sole et luna et sideribus, quorum species manet motu rotabili, et terram et abyssos, quæ velut inconstantes motus patiuntur, atque inferius adjuncta partem alteram numero conferunt ; sed etiam illa quæ aqua et terra produxit potentialiter atque causaliter, priusquam per temporum moras ita exorirentur, quomodo nobis jam nota sunt in eis operibus, quæ Deus usque nunc operatur."

NOTE H. *Part I., chap. vi., p.* 70.

The passages to which I have referred are so characteristic of St. Augustine that I give them both in the original, for the benefit of those who may not be able to refer to his Works.

De Gen. ad Litt., Lib. i. 37.—Having before spoken of the necessity of not being always children in understanding, he adds, "Et in rebus obscuris atque a nostris oculis reconditissimis, si qua inde scripta etiam divina legerimus quæ possint salva fide qua imbuimur, alias atque alias parere sententias; in nullam earum nos præcipiti affirmatione ita projiciamus, ut si forte diligentius discussa veritas eam recte labefactaverit corruamus : non pro sententia divinarum Scripturarum, sed pro nostra ita dimicantes, ut eam velimus Scripturarum esse quæ nostra est ; cum potius eam quæ Scripturarum est, nostram esse velle debeamus. . . .

"39. Plerumque enim accidit ut aliquid de terra, de cœlo, de cæteris mundi hujus elementis, de motu et conversione vel etiam magnitudine et intervallis siderum, de certis defectibus solis ac lunæ, de circuitibus annorum et temporum, de naturis animalium, fruticum, lapidum, atque hujusmodi cæteris, etiam non Christianus ita noverit, ut certissima ratione vel experientia teneat. Turpe est autem nimis et perniciosum ac maxime cavendum, ut christianum de his rebus quasi secundum Christianas Litteras loquentem, ita delirare quilibet infidelis audiat, ut, quemadmodum dicitur, toto cœlo errare conspiciens, risum tenere vix possit. Et non tam molestum est, quod errans homo deridetur, sed quod auctores nostri ab eis qui foris sunt, talia sensisse creduntur, et cum magno eorum exitio de quorum salute satagimus, tanquam indocti reprehenduntur atque respuuntur. . . . Quid enim molestiæ tristitiæque ingerant prudentibus fratribus temerarii præsumptores, satis dici non potest."

NOTE I. *Part I., chap. vi., p.* 71.

De Genesi ad Literam, Lib. V. (v).—"Factæ itaque creaturæ motibus cœperunt currere tempora: unde ante creaturam frustra tempora requiruntur, quasi possint inveniri ante tempora tempora. . . Potius ergo tempus a creatura, quam creatura cœpit a tempore; utrumque autem ex Deo. . . Quapropter cum primam conditionem creaturarum cogitamus, a quibus operibus suis Deus in die septimo requievit; nec illos dies sicut istos solares, nec ipsam operationem ita cogitare debemus, quemadmodum nunc aliquid Deus operatur in tempore; sed quemadmodum operatus est unde inciperent tempora, quemadmodum operatus est omnia simul, præstans eis etiam ordinem, non intervallis temporum sed connexione causarum, ut ea quæ simul facta sunt, senario quoque illius diei numero præsentato perficerentur. Non itaque temporali sed causali ordine prius facta est informis formabilisque materies, et spiritualis et corporalis, de qua fieret quod faciendum esset, cum et ipsa priusquam instituta est, non fuisset: nec instituta est nisi ab illo utique summo Deo et vero, ex quo sunt omnia."

And again after enumerating the works of creation:—

"Hunc omnem ordinem creaturæ ordinatæ dies ille cogno-

Appendix.

vit; et per hanc cognitionem sexies quodammodo præsentatus tanquam sex dies exhibuit, cum sit unus dies, ea quæ facta sunt, in creatore primitus et in ipsis consequenter agnoscens, nec in ipsis remanens, sed eorum etiam cognitionem posteriorem ad Dei referens dilectionem, vesperam et mane et meridiem in omnibus præbuit; non per moras temporum, sed propter ordinem conditorum.

NOTE J. *Part I., chap. vi., p. 75.*

Mivart, who has referred to some of the same passages of St. Augustine as I have quoted, has also noticed that in the mediæval period Thomas Aquinas, and since the Reformation, (or, as he calls it, "the movement of Luther") Suarez, both of them widely venerated as orthodox teachers, have accepted and confirmed the opinions of Augustine as to "potential" or derivative creation. But I have thought it best, instead of examining their writings, to confine my inquiries to those writings of the great Augustine which bear directly on the question at issue.

NOTE K. *Part I., chap. viii., p. 92.*

Et de spinis quidem ac tribulis absolutior potest esse responsio, quia post peccatum dictum est homini de terra, *Spinas et tribulos pariet tibi*; nec tamen facile dicendum est tunc cœpisse ista oriri ex terra. Fortassis enim quoniam in ipsis quoque generibus seminum multæ reperiuntur utilitates, poterant habere locum suum sine ulla pœna hominis. Sed ut in agris in quibus jam pœnaliter laborabat, etiam ista nascerentur, hoc ad cumulum pœnæ valere credi potest, cum possent alibi nasci, vel ad avium pecorumque pastus, vel ad ipsorum hominum aliquos usus. Quanquam et ille sensus non abhorret ab his verbis, quo ita intelligitur dictum, *Spinas et tribulos pariet tibi*, ut hæc etiam antea terra pariens, non tamen homini pareret ad laborem, sed cujuscemodi animalibus convenientem cibum; sunt enim quæ his generibus, et mollioribus et avidioribus, commode suaviterque vescantur: tunc autem cœperit ista homini parere ad ærumnosum negotium, cum post peccatum cœpit in terra laborare. Non quod aliis locis hæc antea nascerentur, et post in agris quos homo ad capiendas fruges coleret; sed et prius et postea in eisdem locis: prius tamen non homini, post autem homini; ut hoc significetur quod additum est, *tibi;* quia non est dictum, Spinos et tribulos pariet, sed, *pariet tibi;* id est, ut tibi jam ista nasci incipiant ad laborem, quæ ad pastum tantummodo aliis animalibus antea nascebatur." It would be difficult to find a passage that more distinctly exhibits the strong tendency of Augustine's mind to treat such questions *rationally*, that is, consistently with the Divine Wisdom, of which the reason given to man is the reflection.

NOTE L. *Part II., chap. ii., p.* 113.

It is, for example, evident that Augustine considered the knowledge of the Creation as inseparable from the reality of its existence. His ignorance of Greek makes it certain that he never studied the philosophy of Aristotle in his original writings, but there can be little doubt that the philosophy which he studied in his youth would have been affected by the "Metaphysics" of Aristotle, who, in his treatise on the "Soul," never separates existence from knowledge. A thing in actual existence, he says, is identical with the knowledge of that thing. Again, "the possible existence of a thing is identical with the possibility in us of perceiving or knowing it." "Aristotle would have considered it very unphilosophical to represent matter as some philosophers of the present day appear to do, as having had an independent existence, and as having contained the germs, not only of all other things, but even of reason itself, so that out of matter Reason was developed. According to Aristotle, it is impossible to conceive matter at all as actually existing," except as realized by Reason.* Augustine's view appears to have been that the knowledge of material things by God gave them their actual existence.

* I quote from Sir Alexander Grant's volume on Aristotle in the series of Ancient Classics for English Readers, p. 165, 167.

NOTE M. *Part II., chap. viii., p.* 189.

The following passage is taken from the Preface to a work on Animal Mechanism, by the Rev. Dr. Haughton, of Trinity College, Dublin; one of the most eminent scientific men of the present day, who does not believe in the theory of Natural Selection as any true cause of the development of the animal kingdom. It will explain how the definitions given by me of the evolution of creation are consistent with the religious truth of the whole being ordered by Divine Wisdom. He says: " In the course of my investigations, I have met with numerous instances, in the muscular mechanism of the vertebrate animals, of the application of the principle of *least action* in Nature; by which I mean that the work to be done is effected by means of the existing arrangement of the muscles, bones, and joints, with a less expenditure of force than would be possible under any other arrangement; so that any alteration would be a positive disadvantage to the animal. If, as I consider probable, this fact should prove to be of much wider occurrence in nature than these instances show, it may serve to give us some slight glimpse of the mechanism by which the conservation of species in nature is secured. In astronomy, the conservation of the solar system depends upon certain well-known conditions regulating the motions of the several bodies of which that system consists; and it is a matter of indifference whether these conditions were directly imposed by the Will of the Divine Contriver, or were the indirect result of some former condition of the system. In either case, these conditions are equally the result of the contrivance. If the present state of the solar system be the result, according to fixed laws, of some pre-existing state of that system, it may be said, in the language of naturalists, to have been evolved out of its former state; but in such an evolution there was nothing left to Chance; it was all foreseen, and the evolution presided over by the Divine Mind that planned the whole. I cannot see why there may not be in organic life a similar process of evolution from lower forms of existence; but it is a teleological evolution, in which every step and every result was foreseen and planned beforehand. The laws of such an evolution appear to me, in the present state of our knowledge, to be entirely unknown." The argument of Dr. Haughton is not in the least affected, even if we allow, as it seems to me we must, that the evolution was to *some extent* modified by "natural selection," and the "survival of the fittest." Indeed, he seems to admit that the principle of least action in animal mechanism would work in the same direction as "survival of the fittest," only as the cause, not as the result.

NOTE N. *Part II., chap. x., p.* 205.

"De Genesi ad Litteram," vi. 36: "Denique non ait Apostolus, corpus quidem mortale propter peccatum; sed *corpus mortuum propter peccatum.* Illud quippe ante peccatum, et mortale secundum aliam, et immortale secundum aliam causam diei poterat: id est, mortale, quia poterat mori; immortale quia poterat non mori. Aliud est enim non posse mori, sicut quasdam naturas immortales creavit Deus; aliud est autem posse non mori, secundum quem modum primus creatus est homo immortalis; quod ei præstabatur de ligno vitæ non de constitutione naturæ. . . Mortalis ergo erat conditione corporis animalis, immortalis autem beneficio Conditoris."

www.ingramcontent.com/pod-product-compliance
Lightning Source LLC
Chambersburg PA
CBHW021939240426
43669CB00047B/558